BRANCH

MEMORIES

(DEVON & CORNWALL – 2)

ERIC R. SHEPHERD

ARK PUBLICATIONS (RAILWAYS)

First published in 2008 by ARK PUBLICATIONS (RAILWAYS), an imprint of Forest Publishing, Woodstock, Liverton, Newton Abbot, Devon TQ12 6JJ

British Library Cataloguing in Publication Data

A catalogue record for this book is available from the British Library

ISBN 978 1 873029 14 5

ARK PUBLICATIONS (RAILWAYS)

Editorial, layout and design by:
Mike Lang

Typeset by:
Carnaby Typesetting, Torquay, Devon TQ1 1EG

Printed and bound in Great Britain by:
The Latimer Trend Group, Plymouth, Devon PL6 7PY

Front cover illustration:

Collett 0–4–2T No. 1427 pulling out of the platform line to pick up a second coach at Ashburton Station in the mid-1950s.
By kind permission of David Elphick

CONTENTS

Introduction   5

1   The Ashburton Branch   7

2   The Bodmin and Wadebridge Railway   31

3   The Brixham Branch   49

4   The Kingsbridge Branch   59

5   The Launceston Branch   75

6   The Teign Valley Branch   103

     Bibliography   125

     The Author   127

     Other Titles available from ARK Publications

     (Railways)   128

ACKNOWLEDGEMENTS

This book, like my earlier volume published in 2005 on the same subject, is largely the result of help and encouragement from my publisher, Mike Lang, for which I am sincerely grateful. Recalling my experiences whilst travelling on these railways has been very pleasurable, and it is to be hoped that they will be of interest to you, the reader.

I am also extremely grateful to David Elphick for allowing his superb painting of 0–4–2T No. 1427 at Ashburton Station to be reproduced on the front cover.

My sincere thanks must also be given to my wife Anne for allowing me to retire to the study over a period of several months during the preparation of the manuscript.

(The photographs are all from my own camera.)

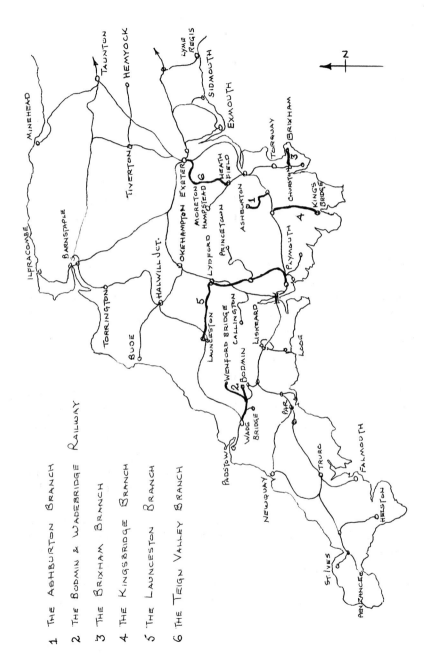

1 THE ASHBURTON BRANCH

2 THE BODMIN & WADEBRIDGE RAILWAY

3 THE BRIXHAM BRANCH

4 THE KINGSBRIDGE BRANCH

5 THE LAUNCESTON BRANCH

6 THE TEIGN VALLEY BRANCH

4

INTRODUCTION

Sixty years ago Devon and Cornwall possessed a considerable number of branch lines, which spread out from the main lines of the Great Western Railway and the Southern Railway to serve a wide variety of towns and villages in the countryside.

Before the growth of road transport, and in an age when it was sometimes necessary to walk a considerable distance to the nearest station, these lines were an essential part of life in rural areas.

My interest in them started at an early age and, having endeavoured to convey some of the enjoyment which I found when travelling along six of the lines featured in an earlier volume (published in 2005), I have now been able to share my memories of another six that particularly appealed to me. As before, I have also attempted to portray their atmosphere and daily working whilst deliberately avoiding the temptation to describe the history of each of the lines in detail.

Of those included in this volume, the Brixham branch was the shortest, at 2 miles, whereas at the other extreme the Launceston branch extended to over 30 miles and passed through at least part of the valleys of no less than eight rivers. Collectively, the scenery from the carriage window varied from pleasant farmland and wooded valleys to uncultivated moorland, whilst not a few stations had gardens which were tended by the staff – often in the hope of gaining an award in the annual competition run by the railway company!

Nowadays only a few branch lines remain in Devon and Cornwall, and even their future is heavily dependant on government policies. Nevertheless, it is pleasing to know that one of those included in this book – the Ashburton branch – has survived, in part at least, and is now operated as a preserved line between Totnes and Buckfastleigh by the South Devon Railway.

Eric R. Shepherd
January 2008

5

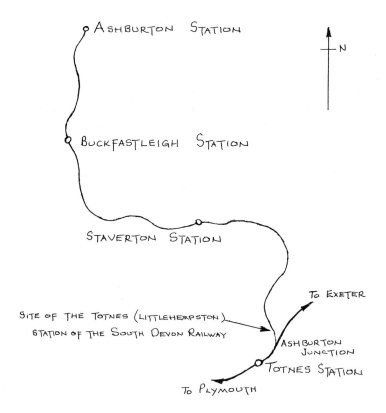

THE ASHBURTON BRANCH

ASHBURTON STATION

N

BUCKFASTLEIGH STATION

STAVERTON STATION

To EXETER

SITE OF THE TOTNES (LITTLEHEMPSTON)
STATION OF THE SOUTH DEVON RAILWAY

ASHBURTON
JUNCTION

TOTNES STATION

To PLYMOUTH

NOT TO SCALE

1. THE ASHBURTON BRANCH

The Totnes to Ashburton line of the Great Western Railway was one of the branches reasonably close to my home in Torquay. It was also of special interest to my family, as my father had told me how, in his younger days, he and his parents would travel over part of it when going to the village of Holne, on Dartmoor, which was a favourite place for their holidays. He had then gone on to describe the journey from Torquay in greater detail and explained that, during the early years of the 20th century, this had entailed first making their way to Torre Station and catching a train to Newton Abbot. From there they would then change to a Plymouth–bound train and travel to Totnes before alighting, crossing the footbridge and boarding the Ashburton branch train. This, in turn, would then enable them to reach Buckfastleigh Station, and here a pony and trap would be waiting to take them to their ultimate destination.

At the time I was intrigued by all this, but it was my father's description of the journey along the little branch line from Totnes, with its views of the River Dart, that really captured my imagination. Furthermore, I determined to visit it at the first possible opportunity and this eventually came in April 1937, when a friend and I were able to purchase '7 Day Runabout' tickets enabling us to travel in an area bounded by Dawlish Warren, Kingswear (and Dartmouth), Kingsbridge, St Budeaux – and Ashburton! The cost of these tickets, incidentally, was 5/- (25p) for under-14s, and during the seven days we covered most of the area, paying special attention to the branch line from Brent to Kingsbridge and, of course, that from Totnes to Ashburton.

I did not record the details of the train in which we travelled to Ashburton. However, I can still remember the journey and also looking at a well-kept garden on the 'up' platform at Totnes Station, which my father had described to me; this incorporated a small pond and fountain, and was a very pleasing feature.

The nameboard and garden on the 'up' platform at Totnes Station.

It was from this same platform that our journey commenced, the little branch train pulling gently out onto the main line and very soon crossing the nearby bridge over the River Dart. The main line was then promptly forsaken for the branch proper at Ashburton Junction, and I recall my youthful excitement at travelling on a 'new' railway as we curved away to the north-west.

Soon, after first having passed under an accommodation bridge, the line curved around more towards the north-east until bringing us right alongside the river that we had crossed a little earlier. The view from the carriage window was then absolutely delightful and, with our train running only a short distance away from the water's edge over the next $1^1/_2$ miles or so, this continued to be very much a feature of this part of the journey. In the meantime, although barely noticeable, the line changed direction yet again as it gently followed the course of the river around to the west, after which the two finally began to part company. Almost coincidentally, the tower of Staverton church loomed up on the northern side of the line, while a few moments later a gated level crossing at 2 miles 56 chains took us over a lane which led to a former mill. (By then the River Dart was a field away, but I was to discover in later years that by way of compensation a fine show of snowdrops appeared beside the line each spring just beyond this point.)

During the course of the next minute or so the river came into sight once more and then, shortly after passing a weir, we arrived at another gated level crossing; this carried the line over a minor road immediately before we entered the confines of Staverton

A train bound for Totnes, consisting of 0–4–2T No. 1470 and auto saloon No. 244, seen approaching the weir shortly after leaving Staverton Station on 8th June 1957.

A deserted Staverton Station, viewed from the level crossing, 24th June 1950.

Station (3 miles 25 chains). Here, apart from a small ground frame cabin just inside the level-crossing gates, all the facilities were on the northern side of the line. These included a relatively short platform, the main station building and two goods sheds, the easternmost of which was served by a siding that went across the same road as the running line in order to reach it.

A whistle from our locomotive echoed across the fields as we drew out of the station and continued up the wide valley in close proximity to the river, presently passing under the Totnes to Buckfastleigh road at Riverford (or Hood) Bridge. A further two miles then brought the train to its second crossing of the river at Nursery Pool Bridge, after which we were soon also crossing the

0–4–2T No. 1470, with auto saloon No. 158, crossing Nursery Pool Bridge on 15th July 1949.

little River Mardle and slowly making our way into Buckfastleigh Station (6 miles 75 chains).

Passing facilities were provided here, and the main station building, with its attendant goods shed, stood on the 'down' platform, whilst a short platform on the 'up' side appeared to be rarely, if ever, used. By contrast, the 'down' platform seemed to me to be unusually long for an intermediate branch line station, but perhaps it was an echo of busier days in past years. The layout was completed with a signal box and sidings at the northern end of the station site.

Buckfastleigh Station, looking towards Ashburton on 24th June 1950.

Our train had been climbing on fairly gentle gradients most of the way from Totnes but, after leaving Buckfastleigh Station and crossing the River Dart for the third time, the remainder of the journey involved considerably steeper gradients as the line followed the valley of a tributary stream – the River Ashburn. Consequently, our locomotive was working quite hard as we passed Pridhamsleigh Farm, with its striking circular dovecote, and was still doing so when we presently ran beneath the Ashburton bypass road towards the end of our journey.

The first sign of the terminus (at 9 miles 37 chains) came when I saw the branch engine shed on the right-hand side of the line, after which we ran gently into the station and halted under its overall wooden roof. From here the passenger platform and main station building were directly to our left, whilst a cattle dock – served by an extension of the run-round loop – was to our right. The goods shed, on the other hand, was situated further to the south, behind the passenger platform, and this was reached by means of a long siding which also served a number of industrial premises.

On this first trip we did not go up into the town, but waited at the station for the return journey, well pleased with our day's excursion. The branch, incidentally, was subjected to an overall speed restriction of 40 miles per hour, and the average journey time for a passenger train was twenty-two minutes.

11

A view from the passenger platform at Ashburton Station looking towards Buckfastleigh. The engine shed can be seen immediately to the right of the water tower, 11th October 1958.

Ashburton Station, looking towards the stop blocks on 24th June 1950, with 0–4–2T No. 1470 and auto saloon No. 189 forming the branch service. The spare saloon standing in the loop siding is No. 192.

Although I did not travel to Ashburton by rail again for a few years, I managed to see the branch train on several occasions in the course of cycling around the area. A favourite ride from my home was via Marldon to Staverton village and on to the station, which adjoined the ancient road bridge over the River Dart.

One such occasion was on 20th April 1940, when 0–4–2T No. 4870 with auto saloon No. 132 formed the branch service, and this same locomotive was seen on two subsequent occasions, first on 17th May 1941 with auto saloon No. 130 and again on 7th November 1942 with auto saloon No. 111. (This little engine was used on the line for many years, and featured during the last day of passenger services under British Railways, by then of course having become No. 1470.)

My second journey on the line took place on 6th February 1943, when a single trip was made from Totnes to Staverton, almost certainly in connection with a walk through the lanes to see the snowdrops which grow in the hedges of the area at that time of the year. The train consisted of auto saloon No. 132 propelled by 0–4–2T No. 4870, which was a familiar pairing, but a cycling visit

to Ashburton on 11th September 1943 brought a surprise. On that day the same auto saloon was coupled to 2–4–0T No. 3582, a rather ancient locomotive which I had not seen before on the line, and never saw again, although of course it may have appeared at other times.

The beginning of 1947 is memorable for a period of heavy snow, and on 22nd February, in order to see the countryside under snow, my family and I went by bus to Totnes and then travelled on the 1.40 p.m. train as far as Staverton.

Passengers for the train journey were accommodated in corridor brake 1st/3rd composite coach No. 7537, which was hauled by 0–4–2T No. 1466.

A view along the line between Staverton and Totnes on 22nd February 1947.

After a walk, we returned on the 4.42 p.m. service to Totnes; as the coach was not fitted for auto working the locomotive had had to run around its train at the terminus, which was an unusual procedure for passenger trains on the line.

The scenery, especially the sections beside the river, made the excursion well worthwhile.

Several rides on the line ensued in the following years, mostly in connection with rambles around the district, and usually with No. 1470 hauling the train, although Nos. 1439, 1427 and 1466 of the same class were noted from time to time, together with, on 1st August 1949, 0–6–0PT No. 7427 and auto saloons Nos. 192 and 158.

When not in use, the second auto saloon was often stabled under the overall wooden roof of Ashburton Station, and during a trip over the whole line on 22nd March 1952 I noted the spare was No. 229. The service train on that day consisted of 0–4–2T No. 1470 coupled to auto saloon No. 192.

On 30th August 1957 a visit to Totnes found the branch train made up of 0–4–2T No. 1427 and auto saloon No. 167, and I realised later that this was the end of an era, as after that date I saw no more branch trains running as auto units.

A subsequent ride over the line on 9th November 1957 was made with 0–4–2T No. 1470 in charge of LMR corridor coach No. 26126 (in dark red livery) and WR corridor coach No. 6066 (in red and cream livery). Passengers were very few and, to our surprise, tickets were collected at Staverton on the return journey from Ashburton. The return fare for the journey was 2/6d. (12^{1}/$_{2}$p).

One of the notices announcing the withdrawal of the passenger service on the branch.

In early October of the following year notices were posted stating that the passenger service was to be withdrawn as from 3rd November 1958. As a result, my family and I decided to have a final, 'normal' ride over the line whilst there was still the opportunity. The chosen date was 11th October, and on our arrival at Totnes we found a single non-corridor coach, No. 6276, standing at the platform with 0–4–2T No. 1427. We rode on the 2.0 p.m. train, which took only nineteen minutes to reach Ashburton, whereas the return trip was more leisurely, at twenty-three minutes.

Less than a month later, on Saturday, 1st November, we drove by car to Totnes Station to witness the 'last day' trains. The first to appear was the 12.15 p.m. from Ashburton, which arrived five minutes late at 12.40 p.m. and consisted of 0–4–2T No. 1470 (clean and in black livery) coupled to non-corridor coaches Nos. 6277 and 2754. The locomotive then ran around her train and took water prior to backing down to collect three additional non-corridor coaches (Nos. 1390 – 2799 – 1848) which were standing in a siding. Meanwhile, we had already noticed 0–4–2T No. 1466 waiting in the goods shed on the opposite side of the main line, and she now came across and coupled up ahead of No. 1470, after which the train drew into the 'up' platform, both locomotives being in reverse. (No. 1466 had also been cleaned for the occasion and looked very smart in her unlined black livery, with the brass of her number plates and the steel of her buffers burnished and shining.)

0–4–2T locomotives Nos. 1466 and 1470 waiting to leave Totnes with the 12.55 p.m., five-coach, train to Ashburton on the last day of the passenger service on the branch, 1st November 1958.

This five-coach train, headed by the pair of '14xx' class locomotives (a *most* unusual occurrence), eventually pulled out of the station at 1.5 p.m., ten minutes after the advertised departure time; the first two coaches were quite well filled, but the rest of the train held very few passengers.

Following the train's departure, we had a snack lunch in Totnes and returned to the station in time to see the arrival, a few minutes late, of the 1.45 p.m. branch train, with a fair passenger complement. After the locomotives had run around their coaches, the 2.0 p.m. train left at 2.17 p.m., once more with a reasonable number of passengers, as was the case with all the trains on that day.

Our next move was by car to Staverton Station, where we saw

the 3.0 p.m. train arrive from Ashburton and collect a few waiting local inhabitants before leaving again at 3.9 p.m. We then continued in the car to Ashburton, pausing at Buckfastleigh to see the 3.41 p.m. arrive and depart for Ashburton.

Two more photographs of the 'last day' trains in the charge of 0–4–2T locomotives Nos. 1466 and 1470:–
Above: The 3 p.m. train departing from Staverton Station en route to Totnes.

Below: The 3.41 p.m. train leaving Buckfastleigh Station en route to Ashburton.

At the terminus we watched the 4.15 p.m. leave in the fading light of the winter's afternoon before returning to Totnes to see its arrival there and subsequent departure, on time, at 4.55 p.m., the majority of passengers appearing to be whistling and shouting teenagers.

After a break for tea, we returned to the station once more in time to greet the 6.7 p.m. working, which drew into the 'down' platform only five minutes behind schedule; the passengers included the Portreeve of Ashburton, who was wearing his chain of office. This train then waited until the 6.34 p.m. 'up' main line stopping train had departed before moving across to the 'up' side in readiness to provide the last service to Ashburton.

In the meantime, having already purchased tickets for this trip, we had joined the sizeable crowd on the 'up' platform and were now able to take our seats in the second coach, No. 6277. After that, we were soon on the move, the train pulling out of Totnes Station on time, at 6.45 p.m., with the locomotives sounding both their whistles (each tone separately in succession) and to the accompaniment of some exploding detonators. By now, of course, darkness had descended and as we approached Ashburton Junction it could be seen that the signal lamps there showed two reds, a white and, on the extreme left, a green for our train. Moments later, as we curved onto the branch metals, it could also be seen that many heads were leaning out of the carriage windows along the length of the train.

At the level crossing by the former mill near Staverton there was more whistling, and at Staverton Station a handful of people awaited us on the platform. Several fireworks were thrown from the train before we departed at 6.53 p.m. with yet more whistling from the locomotives.

On reaching Buckfastleigh, we received a somewhat muted welcome as there were only about half a dozen people on the platform to greet us. We left again at 7.4 p.m. and presently announced our arrival on the outskirts of Ashburton with more use of the whistles; this was answered by people waving from the lighted windows of their houses.

When our train arrived at the terminus, at 7.9 p.m., there was a fairly large crowd of people on the platform, and this was soon augmented by the many passengers alighting after their last ride up the line. We, of course, were included amongst their number but, unlike the majority of them who had now reached journey's end, we and several others were contemplating the trip back to Totnes; this was a special working in order to take the train off the branch, but one on which passengers were permitted to travel.

As we waited in eager anticipation, the train presently reversed a short distance, the two locomotives uncoupled, ran around their coaches and coupled up at the rear before drawing forwards to the platform once more. We were then allowed to rejoin the train and four minutes later, at 7.33 p.m., we were on the move again, with whistles sounding as far as the bridge under the Ashburton bypass road. After that, it was not long at all before we were rolling into Buckfastleigh Station, where a few passengers detrained and where there were still only half a dozen or so people to see us pass.

More whistling marked our departure at 7.41 p.m., and this was repeated at Staverton, where about a dozen people saw us leave at 7.50 p.m. No tickets were collected here, and we ran gently down the valley as far as the 'home' signal at Totnes, where we were held for a short while. When the green signal was given, we pulled quietly into the 'down' platform with only two short whistles, coming to rest at 8.0 p.m.

As we alighted, people were clustered around the locomotives talking to the crews, and we left the station thinking that we had travelled on the branch for the very last time. It also seemed that the name 'Bulliver', as the locals had called their train for many years, would now become a thing of the past. Indeed, about the only small crumb of comfort was the fact that the line was being kept open for the branch goods train, which ran on Mondays to Fridays each week and was, by now, usually headed by a '45xx' class 2–6–2T.

Unfortunately, after less than four more years, and because of dwindling amounts of traffic, the parcels and freight facilities on the branch were also withdrawn, the line being officially closed to all traffic on 10th September 1962 – a little over ninety years after it had been opened. As a result, the last goods train ran on Friday, 7th September and, after the Plymouth Railway Circle had run a farewell special over the line on the following day, consisting of thirteen brake vans hauled by 2–6–2T No. 4567, the branch fell silent.

At the time it was assumed that the track would soon be lifted and the branch left to nature. However, later that same month it was unexpectedly announced in the local press that a group of fourteen professional and business men were working on a plan to reopen the line on a commercial basis by operating steam trains as a tourist attraction, principally between June and September each year. To me, this was excellent news and I awaited further developments with great anticipation!

In the event, the formalities of transferring the ownership of the line from British Railways proved to be a long and complicated process, not helped by the fact that most of the section from Buckfastleigh to Ashburton was earmarked by the Ministry of Transport to form a new stretch of the A38 main road. However, whilst the negotiations continued, the prospective purchasers first of all formed a private company (the Dart Valley Light Railway Company Limited) and then obtained permission for selected rolling stock to travel down the branch from Totnes to Buckfastleigh for storage, the first consignment, which included ex-GWR locomotives 0–6–0 No. 3205 and 2–6–2T No. 4555, arriving there on 2nd October 1965. By that stage it was already clearly evident that there were numerous tasks to be undertaken in order to prepare the railway for its new life, and, fortunately, there were many railway enthusiasts who wished to take part in this work. As a result, working parties were set up and eventually, on 22nd October 1966, the Dart Valley Railway Association was formed as an official body of volunteer supporters: the occasion was marked by the running of a special train consisting of 2–6–2T No. 4555 and three chocolate and cream-liveried auto saloons, which made two trips to Ashburton and back from Buckfastleigh.

In 1968, with work continuing on bringing the railway and its infrastructure up to scratch, the negotiations with British Railways finally led to the new company completing the purchase of the line and its buildings from a point just short of the junction at the Totnes end to Buckfastleigh Station, a distance of some 7 miles. (It was unfortunate that the whole line could not have been included, but at least the most picturesque part of its route was now safeguarded for the future.) Despite this significant development, though, the company was still unable to carry fare-paying passengers as it had not yet been granted a Light Railway Order from the Ministry of Transport. Consequently, a further delay ensued whilst the matter was finalised and it was not until the following spring that the company was able to announce that a service of public passenger trains would be inaugurated on Saturday, 5th April.

Much to my disappointment I was unable to attend on that day, but three weeks later, on 26th April, my family and I travelled to Buckfastleigh Station in our car eager to see how this rejuvenated railway was faring. We then purchased our tickets (the fare was 6/6d. – 32p) before boarding the waiting train, which was formed by ex–GWR locomotive 0–6–0PT No. 6435 and a pair of auto saloons. After that, it was not long before the departure time of 1.45 p.m. arrived and we were able to sit back and enjoy the gentle pace of the journey as the train ran down the valley, the fresh spring greenery enhancing the view from the windows of our carriage.

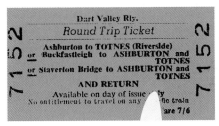

Staverton Station was very trim, with a fine show of polyanthus on the platform, and all too soon the end of the journey came as we reached the 'outer home' signal guarding the junction with the main line outside Totnes Station. At that time, of course, there were no facilities at this point and passengers had to remain on the train; after a wait of seven minutes, the return journey commenced with the driver at his controls in the leading auto coach and the fireman by himself in the locomotive as it propelled the train.

We arrived back at Buckfastleigh feeling very pleased that we had been able to ride on the branch once again, a thing which had not seemed possible on that sombre day in November 1958. Before leaving, we also looked around the station area and noted the following locomotives, all GWR types, which were then currently on site:–

0–6–0PTs Nos. 1369 – 1638 – 6412 – 6430, 0–4–2Ts Nos. 1420 – 1450, and 2–6–2T No. 4555.

This visit was the first of many which have subsequently been made, and the next of several dates to stand out in my memory is 18th October 1969. On that occasion, during a visit to Staverton Station, I saw a special train of seven coaches carrying members of the line's supporters being hauled by 0–6–0PT No. 1638 (complete with an 'AGM' headboard), with 2–6–2T No. 4555 at the rear.

Another date that comes to mind in the early days of the line under private ownership is 2nd October 1971, when I paid a visit to Ashburton Station. Although the new owners were not permitted to work regular passenger trains to the former terminus,

The seven-coach 'D.V.R.A. AGM Special' seen leaving Staverton Station on 18th October 1969, headed by 0–6–0PT No. 1638 and with 2–6–2T No. 4555 at the rear.

The return working of the 'D.V.R.A. AGM Special', seen here approaching Staverton Station.

they were allowed to run special trains there from time to time, and this was one such instance. Sadly, though, on this occasion it was to mark the abandonment of the top part of the line prior to the track being lifted to make way for the new A38 main road, and at 3.5 p.m. I saw what I was told was the last-ever passenger working to leave Ashburton; it consisted of a long train of blue and grey BR coaches attached to 2–6–2T No. 4588 which, by then, was in private ownership.

The last-ever (?) passenger working to leave Ashburton, depicted here on the outskirts of the town.

For various reasons I did not pay a further visit to the railway for several years. However, during that period work was put in hand to construct a completely new station at the Totnes end of the line, which was initially called Totnes Riverside and consisted of a run-round loop line and a platform. Consequently, once the platform was in situ, passengers could alight from trains at this point but were still unable to go anywhere due to the nearby River Dart forming a natural barrier.

Later, in 1985, British Railways somewhat unexpectedly put forward a scheme whereby the branch trains would at long last be allowed access to the main line station at Totnes.

The proposal was accepted, and the new 'through' service commenced with high hopes of an increase in passenger numbers. This was welcome news indeed and, in order to ride over this section of line once again, my family and I joined the 12.10 p.m. train at Totnes Station on 25th July 1985, travelling in one of six corridor coaches hauled by a sparklingly clean 2–6–2T No. 4555. As we pulled out from the platform it was difficult to realise that twenty-seven years had elapsed since that last journey in November 1958!

However, this arrangement was terminated after only three years due to the extra remuneration from passenger fares being exceeded by the costs incurred in using the main line and BR station. As a result, all journeys on the branch from Buckfastleigh once more ended at Totnes Riverside, which was still being developed and now known as Littlehempston Riverside in order to avoid giving passengers the impression that they could gain access from there to the nearby town.

In 1990 a major change took place concerning the operation of the line, when the Dart Valley Light Railway Company, who had also taken over the Paignton to Kingswear line in 1972, decided that the Buckfastleigh enterprise was losing money and suggested that the Dart Valley Railway Association (the volunteer group) took over its operation.

The changeover to leasing the railway involved several legal complications, but these were successfully resolved in time for the newly formed South Devon Railway Trust to take over the leases of the line and workshops from the beginning of 1991. In addition, the supporters' association – renamed the South Devon Railway Association – continued to provide invaluable volunteer assistance in many departments.

As well as running its normal passenger services, the railway, on occasions, played host to visiting locomotives, and this practice still continues. One such instance which I witnessed was on 13th June 1992, when the famous GWR 4–4–0 No. 3440 *City of Truro* worked a passenger train.

Similar highlights are special Gala Days, with intensive train services, which attract large numbers of visitors.

A very popular event which takes place outside the normal summer timetable is the operation, in the Christmas season, of the 'Santa by Steam' trains. This is an experience which has been enjoyed by the younger members of our family, extending over several years from 1999. On each visit the decorated train of seven coaches was hauled by 0–6–0 No. 3205, complete with an appropriate headboard on its smokebox. One coach contained

'Santa's Grotto', and the destination board on its side read 'North Pole'!

The train was patrolled by characters such as 'Dr Foster' and 'Wee Willie Winkie' before the arrival of Santa himself, who invited all the children into his 'Grotto' to receive their presents. A good time was had by all, and long may these special trains continue to run!

The day-to-day trains on the line in BR days were, as we have seen, worked mainly as a single-saloon auto train, but even a two-coach formation would be insufficient for passengers using the line in today's busy holiday season and this is why longer trains are used on most services. However, on occasions such as Gala Days a '14xx' class 0–4–2T with two auto saloons is fitted into the timetable, and this train stops at the tiny Napper's Halt below Staverton village.

The platform here is almost at rail level, and on 5th April 1999, whilst standing by the adjacent level crossing, we saw the auto train arrive from the Buckfastleigh direction, with 0–4–2T No. 1420 and auto saloons Nos. 225 and 228. Then, after it had stopped, the door of the saloon opposite the tiny platform opened and the guard lowered the retractable steps to allow several passengers to alight – a real echo of former branch line operation! (The village of Staverton, with its church and Sea Trout Inn, is only a short walk away and an interesting place to pass the time before the return train is due at the halt.)

With this sort of attention to detail, combined with the friendly service, it was hardly surprising that the arrangement whereby the South Devon Railway Trust had taken over the railway in 1991 had already proved to be very successful. By now, though, the management had become only too well aware that the two leases would expire early in the 21st century, which meant that no long-term plans could be made for further development. As a result, it was decided in 2001 to make an offer of New Ordinary Shares in a newly formed company – South Devon Railway Plc – in order to raise funds to assist the Trust with the purchase of the line and associated property and thereby safeguard the railway's future: the outcome was a very satisfactory response, which allowed the purchase to proceed, and this was finalised in March 2002.

Since then, and in the years from when the railway was first taken over from BR, a continuous process of improvement has taken place. A detailed description of this is not appropriate here, but the following list gives some idea of the works which have been, or are being, carried out over and above the routine maintenance requirements of a 7-mile-long railway:–

At the Totnes end of the line

1. Provision of a run-round loop line and sidings.
2. Construction of a completely new station, with equipment obtained from closed parts of the former GWR system.
3. Provision of a new signal box and signalling.
4. Installation of a water supply and water tower.
5. With assistance from other organisations, the erection of a footbridge over the River Dart, giving access to the BR station and the town.

At the Staverton Station area

1. Provision of a passing loop line.
2. Provision of a new signal box and signalling.

At the Buckfastleigh Station area

1. Reorganisation of the layout following the loss of part of the site during the construction of the re-routed A38 main road.
2. Installation of a footbridge giving access to the workshop and leisure areas.
3. Construction of locomotive/carriage sheds and repair shops, with public viewing gallery.
4. Provision of a new signal box and signalling.
5. Installation of a water supply and water tower.
6. Provision of a large car park for visitors.

The initial reason for which visitors come to the railway is probably to take a journey along the line, but Buckfastleigh Station has a great deal of interest, including a model and souvenir shop, an extensive model railway and a café serving hot and cold meals.

The former goods shed houses a museum containing memorabilia of the line, and also the only remaining broad-gauge locomotive (as distinct from replicas) in the form of *Tiny*, a diminutive vertical-boilered shunting engine.

A walk over the footbridge leads to the carriage/locomotive

sheds and repair shop, whilst nearby is a separate building housing a locomotive and wagon from the former Lee Moor Tramway which had the unusual gauge of 4 feet 6 inches.

Two photographs taken at Buckfastleigh Station in more recent times:–
Above: The station as seen from the footbridge.

Below: A view from the 'down' platform looking towards Totnes. Note the approaching pump trolley!

In addition to the ex-GWR locomotives present on the line, there are several of the industrial type, and a small fleet of diesel locomotives and multiple unit trains.

Another attraction is a miniature railway which encircles part of the site, and there is a riverside walk beside the River Dart.

Also run as separate attractions, and reached from the car park, are a butterfly farm and an otter sanctuary, whilst a similar feature at the other end of the line, opposite the station, is a Rare Breeds Centre .

For the more 'hands-on' visitor, the railway can arrange locomotive driving courses or, more sedately, dining trains or even your own train for a special occasion, and of course, on very special occasions, a 'Thomas the Tank Engine' day for the children.

'Thomas the Tank Engine' (ex-LMS 0–6–0T) at Buckfastleigh Station, seen here with the author's wife and granddaughter.

An interesting feature of today's trains is the fact that they take much longer to travel along the line than those which operated in BR days! Whereas a trip from Buckfastleigh to Totnes was timetabled as fifteen minutes, the timing now is a full half an hour, the reason being, of course, that a tourist railway must allow its passengers to admire as much of the lineside scenery as possible.

Even slower is the outward run of the 'Santa by Steam' trains, this being deliberate in order that all the children receive their

0–6–0 No. 3205, on a 'Santa by Steam' train, running around its coaches at Totnes Littlehempston Station.

presents from Santa before the train reaches Totnes Littlehempston (formerly Littlehempston Riverside) Station. No-one objects!

As one of the principal holiday attractions in the area, and after several occasions when its future seemed to hang in the balance, the railway can now look ahead with growing confidence, supported by its staff and loyal volunteers.

Apart from providing trains for tourists, it also plays a vital role in being able to recreate the atmosphere of a rural branch line of the Great Western Railway, which, to those of us who remember such lines, is a source of great pleasure. My most recent experience of that pleasure was on 22nd May 2006, when my wife and I joined the waiting 10.45 a.m. train at Buckfastleigh Station. We found a comfortable compartment in the five-coach train, which was headed by an immaculate-looking 0–6–0PT No. 5786.

Soon after leaving, we crossed the recently rebuilt Nursery Pool Bridge and ran beside the river, which was running high after heavy rain during the previous day. The scenery was as green and peaceful as ever, and all too soon we arrived at Totnes Littlehempston Station.

On the return journey, riding in the rear compartment of the last coach, we could catch glimpses of our locomotive nosing around the curves ahead, whilst now and again wisps of steam drifted past the carriage window.

The South Devon Railway is one not to be missed – if you have not yet ridden beside the River Dart, through scenery which cannot be reached by road, then go and see for yourself!

*****

2. THE BODMIN AND WADEBRIDGE RAILWAY

The Bodmin and Wadebridge Railway was one of the earlier lines in Cornwall and the first in the county to use steam locomotives from its inception in 1834. Apart from linking the two towns named in its title, the railway also had freight-only branches to Ruthern Bridge and Wenford Bridge.

Later, in 1846, the railway was purchased by the London & South Western Railway Company even though, at the time, that company's main line from Waterloo was still around 200 miles away. In fact, the railway remained in isolation from the rest of the L & SWR's system until 1895, when the company's North Cornwall line to Padstow finally reached Wadebridge and began to share the same station as that used for the line to Bodmin. Meanwhile, in 1888, the Great Western Railway Company had obtained running powers over the passenger line from Boscarne Junction to Wadebridge as an extension of its then recently opened branch from Bodmin Road to Bodmin and Boscarne, thus increasing the amount of traffic passing over the lower part of the original railway quite considerably.

My first visit to the Bodmin and Wadebridge Railway came almost exactly one hundred years after its opening when, during a family holiday at Launceston, we caught the 10.51 a.m. train to Wadebridge on 1st September 1934 and then continued to the Southern Railway station at Bodmin in another train hauled by '02' class 0–4–4T No. 221.

Later in the day we returned to Launceston by the same route, but not before discovering that on the 5th and 6th of September an exhibition was to be held at Wadebridge to commemorate the centenary of the Bodmin line.

Deciding that this was an occasion not to be missed, on 5th September we again boarded the mid-morning train to Wadebridge, where we witnessed the arrival of a train from Bodmin headed by '02' class 0–4–4T No. 216, adorned with a string

31

of flags draped around her smokebox.

The exhibition that we had come to see consisted of various items relating to the railway, and two modern coaches were standing open for inspection in the station yard, one of which I think was a kitchen car vehicle. Whilst there, and for the first time, we also saw two of the trio of 2–4–0 Beattie well tank locomotives which were shedded at Wadebridge to work the sharply curved

THE BODMIN AND WADEBRIDGE RAILWAY

Southern Railway
Bodmin and Wadebridge
Railway Centenary
Excursions to
Wadebridge
September 5th & 6th

FROM	DEPART							Third Class Return Fare
	a.m.	a.m.	a.m.	a.m.	p.m.	p.m.	p.m.	s. d.
Padstow	8. 2	8.35	9.12	9.40	12.38 4A30	2.17 5.46	2.50 6.32	9.
Bodmin	7.27	9. 0	11.28		2. 5	4.23	5.39	6.
Dunmere Halt	7.30	9. 3	11.31		2. 9	4.26	5.42	6.
Nanstallon Halt	7.33	9. 6	11.34		2.13	4.29	5.45	6.
Grogley Halt	7.38	9.11	11.39		2.18	4.34	5.50	6.

"A" - Wednesday, 5th September, only.

RETURN SAME DAY BY ANY ORDINARY TRAIN.

CHILDREN UNDER 14 YEARS OF AGE HALF FARE.

NOTICE AS TO CONDITIONS.- These tickets are issued at less than the ordinary fares and are subject to the Notice and Conditions shown in the current time tables.

E1/39053/6.
29/8/34.

H. A. WALKER,
General Manager.

The centenary celebrations also included excursions to Wadebridge as shown on the leaflet reproduced above.

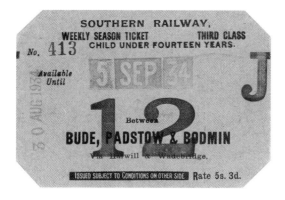

freight-only branch to Wenford Bridge. These survivors from a class of engines dating back to the 1870s were built in 1874 and, at the time of our visit, were numbered 0314 and 3298.

A description of the route of the Bodmin line necessarily commences at Wadebridge, where the main station buildings were situated on the 'down' platform, not far from the goods shed and sidings in the station yard. Opposite the 'down' platform, and connected to it by means of a footbridge, was an island platform from which 'up' trains departed, those bound for Bodmin usually leaving from the far (northern) side. Between the island platform and the nearby River Camel were further sidings, together with a two-road engine shed and turntable.

From the station to the point where the North Cornwall line diverged from the Bodmin and Wadebridge Railway, there were two lines of rail, which, to all intents and purposes, looked like a section of double track. They were, however, two separate single lines, that on the right (southern side) being for Bodmin trains and that on the left being for trains operating on the North Cornwall line.

Beyond this point the Bodmin line ran a little to the east of south and was soon crossing the River Camel at Pendavey Bridge before starting to follow its course upstream in a narrowing wooded valley. Here, at the lower end of the valley and 1 mile 40 chains from Wadebridge, the train passed a derelict platform on the right-hand side, this being known as Shooting Range Platform after having been built to serve a 19th century rifle range.

A little over a mile further on, with the line now running close to the river, the appearance of a disused cutting* on the right-hand side of the train coincided with the approach to Grogley Halt. Situated at 2 miles 72 chains from Wadebridge, this lay just beyond a gentle curve and had a single platform, also on the right-hand side. (The halt formerly had a pagoda shelter, but a more modern shelter and platform were installed in later years.)

Once past Grogley Halt the line gradually swung around to a more easterly direction as it continued up the valley, presently passing a siding on the right-hand side. By that stage the train was also approaching a level crossing, and here, on the left-hand side, stood the platform of Nanstallon Halt (4 miles 32 chains) with its

*The disused cutting had once formed part of the freight-only branch to Ruthern Bridge (4 miles 6 chains), but this had been closed and the track lifted shortly before my first visit in 1934.

pagoda shelter. After that, a short run of just 27 chains brought the train to Boscarne Junction, where the Great Western line diverged to the south on its way to that company's station at the higher part of Bodmin town. In addition, there were several loop sidings here.

Grogley Halt, 26th February 1962.

Nanstallon Halt, 26th February 1962.

Continuing its journey, the train now proceeded to make a second crossing of the river and then, immediately on reaching the other side, arrived at another junction. This was Dunmere Junction (5 miles 7 chains), the point at which the freight-only branch to Wenford Bridge diverged to the north and began to wind its way up the Camel valley. (This branch was over $6^1/_2$ miles long and had resulted in its terminus not only being 11 miles 63 chains from Wadebridge, but also becoming – in 1895 – the furthest point on the L & SWR's system from London's Waterloo Station, which was some 266 miles away!)

A view of Dunmere Junction showing 2–4–0 Beattie well tank locomotive No. 30585 leaving for Boscarne Junction with a clay train on 10th March 1960.

In direct contrast to the freight-only branch, the passenger line began to part company with the river valley beyond Dunmere Junction, from where it was only a very short distance to Dunmere Halt; this consisted of a single platform on the left-hand side of the line with, once again, a pagoda shelter. Then, after passing under the main Bodmin to Wadebridge road, the line rose quite steeply as it continued past Bodmin Gaol and approached the terminus at Bodmin (6 miles 51 chains) on a gradient of 1 in 40.

Unlike Wadebridge, the station at Bodmin had only a single platform which, together with the main buildings, were to the left and on the opposite side of the line from three sidings and a goods shed. The station also boasted a granite milepost of the original railway company, which passengers would walk past and which carried the letters 'M', 'F', 'C' and 'Y' as well as the numbers (one below each letter) '6', '7', '3' and '8' to indicate, very meticulously, the distance from Wadebridge in miles, furlongs, chains and yards!

Dunmere Halt, 10th March 1960.

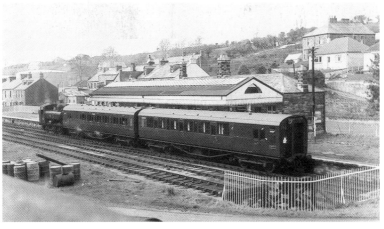

The former Southern Railway terminus at Bodmin, showing ex-GWR 0–6–0PT No. 4666 waiting to leave with the 2 p.m. train to Wadebridge on 10th March 1960.

2–4–0 Beattie well tank locomotive No. 30586 at Wadebridge, 10th March 1960.

Apart from a brief visit to Wadebridge on 13th April 1957, when I saw all three 2–4–0 Beattie well tank locomotives (now with their BR numbers: 30585–30586–30587), my next visit to the Bodmin line took place on 25th May 1957. On that day I arrived at the former Southern Railway station at Bodmin, by then renamed 'Bodmin North', and purchased a day return ticket to Wadebridge at a cost of 1/8d. (8p).

In the yard 2–6–0 No. 31849 was shunting wagons, but presently departed ahead of the waiting passenger train, which consisted of two green-liveried corridor coaches headed by '02' class 0–4–4T No. 236, now renumbered 30236. My journey commenced at 2.0 p.m., and the train coasted down to Dunmere Halt, which had recently been repainted in Western Region colours. At Boscarne Junction we overtook No. 31849 and her train waiting in the loop, and continued to Wadebridge, where the '02' came off and was replaced by 2–6–0 No. 31845 and 'T9' class 4–4–0 No. 30715, the two locomotives double-heading the two-coach train away to Padstow.

I later returned at 3.28 p.m. on an ex-GWR two-coach train headed by 2–6–2T No. 5502, which took me through to the former GWR station at Bodmin (now renamed 'Bodmin General') without stopping at the intermediate halts.

A further visit to Bodmin North Station nearly three years later, on 10th March 1960, revealed that the little '02' class 0–4–4T locomotives had been withdrawn from the line and the two-coach train was now headed by an ex-GWR 0–6–0PT, No. 4666.

Other locomotives of the same type subsequently seen on this duty were No. 4694 on 20th March 1961 and No. 3671 on 26th February 1962.

The following year, 1963, brought a red-letter day on 27th April when, accompanied by my wife and young daughter, I drove to Wadebridge Station to see a special train named the 'North Cornishman' arrive from Exeter. This train, with three coaches, was hauled by preserved 'T9' class 4–4–0 locomotive No. 120, which had been repainted in its former light green livery of the London & South Western Railway.

In conjunction with this train I knew that another train, the 'Camel Valleyman', was to take passengers up the freight-only line to Wenford Bridge, and had managed to obtain a ticket for this, to me, very special journey. I also knew that the Beattie well tank locomotives had finally been withdrawn from service in 1962 and was rather intrigued to see which type of locomotive had arrived to replace them.

The question was quickly answered as the 'Camel Valleyman' drew into the platform, for it was headed by ex-GWR 0–6–0PT No. 1369 – spotlessly clean in black livery with her safety valve bonnet polished and buffers and hose connections brightened with aluminium paint. Her train was made up with twelve goods brake vans, two of these being bogie vehicles; one was No. 56302 and the other, which my wife and daughter boarded in order to keep me a 'place' (brake vans were not noted for 'seats') whilst I admired the locomotive, was No. 56287.

A little later, just as they were about to disembark, one of the train marshals walked by and enquired if they were travelling. They said they were not, but, when he said "you can if you like", my young daughter accepted with alacrity!

We were timed to depart at 1.45 p.m., but were waved away a few minutes late, with No. 1369 proudly displaying a 'Camel Valleyman' headboard on the front of her smokebox.

The train rumbled gently up the valley, reaching Boscarne Junction at 2.2 p.m., and here we were held to allow a train from Bodmin North to come through. A change then became evident, as instead of an ex-GWR 0–6–0PT heading the two-coach train, the locomotive was an Ivatt 2–6–2T, No. 41320.

39

Two photographs of the 'Camel Valleyman', 27th April 1963:–
Above: Ex-GWR 0–6–0PT No. 1369 bringing the brake van special from the
    sidings at Wadebridge.

Below: No. 1369 being replenished at Pencarrow water tank.

After its departure, we reversed to the signal box nearby and then drew forward towards Dunmere Junction in order to take the Wenford Bridge line, subsequently halting again at the approach to the level crossing over the main Bodmin to Wadebridge road. After a pause, the locomotive took her train across the road, protected by a flagman, and we entered the wooded section of the trip, following the winding course of the River Camel. This was a scene far removed from normal train journeys as we passed through an avenue of trees, in places arching over the track, with lineside violets, primroses and wood sorrel in abundance and the river flowing on our left sparkling in the sunshine.

After a while, we passed the site of Penhargard Siding and a few minutes later, at 2.41 p.m., halted at Pencarrow water tank, where No. 1369 was replenished by means of a supply taken from a nearby stream. The passengers were permitted to alight here, and many cameras recorded the scene before we moved off again at 2.56 p.m.

The train presently emerged from the woods and negotiated a sharp curve to the east as it passed through a narrow gap between two cottages to cross a minor road at Hellandbridge (8 miles 12 chains). There was formerly a siding here, one of several on the line originally described as 'wharves', with a 'wharfinger' in charge of affairs. Surely a name from the days of the canals?

We now had a five-minute stop before resuming the journey and presently passing Tresarrett 'wharf' (10 miles 28 chains), where there still was a siding, on that day holding seven vans. Then, after about another mile, we reached the clay processing plant (near Poley's Bridge) which supplied most of the traffic for the line. In fact, we could see several wagons waiting to be loaded as we passed through on our way to completing the final half a mile to Wenford Bridge Depôt (11 miles 63 chains), ultimately arriving there at 3.38 p.m. – some eighteen minutes late. However, time seemed to be of little concern on this truly rural railway; after all, we had taken just under two hours to cover just over 11 miles!

The brake vans quickly emptied and the cameramen got busy once more, whilst a complicated shunting movement took place to reverse the train, which was too long for the run-round loop. After the rear van had been hand-shunted, the locomotive was able to run around the train, which was then temporarily halved and placed in two sidings. The odd van was finally hand-shunted to the rear of the reassembled train, and departure time came at 4.7 p.m., some thirty-two minutes behind schedule.

41

The original granite milepost inscribed '12' at Wenford Bridge Depôt. Note the feint traces of the long-disused siding going across the adjoining road.

Another photograph of the 'Camel Valleyman', shown here departing from Wenford Bridge.

Whilst all this was in progress I looked around the depôt and noticed an original granite milepost inscribed '12', which was sited under the buffer stops of one of the sidings. Another siding, long disused, led across a road and curved to the lower end of the cable-worked incline of a private tramway leading to the De Lank granite quarries, which formerly despatched much stone by rail.

The return ride down the line was as enjoyable as the outward one, the train again stopping for water at the Pencarrow tank. At that date further stone mileposts were to be seen beside the track – I wonder if they are still there?

A memory of the wooded section is seeing the steam from No. 1369 lifting and dissolving above our heads in the greenery of the trees as we continued to the Dunmere level crossing, which was reached at 4.55 p.m.

The ritual of crossing the main road took a few minutes and then we ran on past Dunmere Junction and halted at Boscarne Junction. After receiving 'Line clear', we set off again at 5.8 p.m. and travelled at a much faster pace, evidently trying to recover some lost time, but with a fusillade of smuts from our locomotive's chimney as a result! We finally drew into Wadebridge Station at 5.21 p.m., just twenty-five minutes late after a very memorable afternoon.

In March of the following year (1964) I found that the Ivatt 2–6–2Ts were still in charge of the Bodmin North to Wadebridge passenger trains, but that the trains to and from Bodmin General were being hauled by 63xx diesel locomotives, No. D6307 being recorded on this duty on 31st March.

Major alterations came into force in the summer of 1964 when two exchange platforms were erected at Boscarne and a 4-wheel railbus, No. 79977, was employed to run a shuttle service from there to Bodmin North Station. On 20th June 1964 this unit was also seen making connections at Boscarne with the Bodmin General to Wadebridge trains, now operated with single-car diesel unit 55001.

Later that year, on 19th September, I was lucky enough to have a second trip to Wenford Bridge in what was another brake van special named the '130 Years of Steam'. Organised to commemorate the opening of the line in 1834, this train was made up with fifteen vans (my family and friends were in No. 953604) and once again the locomotive was the faithful No. 1369.

Leaving at 1.16 p.m., we eventually reached our destination at

Ex-GWR 0–6–0PT No. 1369, on the '130 Years of Steam' brake van special, seen crossing the main road at Dunmere (*above*) and stationary for a photo session in Dunmere Woods (*below*).

No. 1369 shunting at Wenford Bridge during the '130 Years of Steam' trip on 19th September 1964.

3.45 p.m., and, after more complicated shunting manoeuvres, began the return trip at 4.10 p.m. It was a fine, sunny afternoon and I spent part of the journey sitting (quite illegally!) on the concrete 'flat' outside the body of the van. We returned to Wadebridge Station at 6.5 p.m., after nearly five hours of enjoyment. And the cost? 6/– (30p)!

At the beginning of 1967 I learned that the train service along the original Bodmin and Wadebridge Railway was to be withdrawn as from 30th January 1967. As a result, I decided that I should take my family for a last, 'normal' ride over the line whilst there was still the opportunity, and on 13th January we duly set off for Bodmin North Station with this in mind. We were, however, somewhat taken aback on our arrival there, as we were greeted with a most depressing scene: some sidings were partially lifted, those that remained had condemned wagons in them and the station itself was in a generally poor condition. Nevertheless, at 1.15 p.m. the 4-wheel railbus No. 79977 arrived from Boscarne and eventually left at 2.0 p.m. with ourselves and four other passengers. Down at Boscarne, steps were lowered and we then descended to the one-sleeper-high platform before walking across to steps which led to a normal height platform on the other line.

After a four-minute wait, single-car diesel unit 55017 arrived from Bodmin General and we were able to find a front seat, which gave us a good view of the line on the way to Wadebridge. Later in the day we returned on the same unit to Bodmin General Station, where we alighted and made our way back to the car.

2nd - SINGLE		SINGLE - 2nd
	Wadebridge to	
Wadebridge		Wadebridge
Bodmin General		Bodmin General
or North		or North
BODMIN GENERAL or NORTH		
(W)	2/0 Fare 2/0	(W)
For conditions see over		For conditions see over

A fortnight later, on 28th January, we were again at Bodmin North Station and found the railbus No. 79977 forming the service when it arrived at 4.30 p.m. from Boscarne; it was packed full and with some passengers (many of them railway enthusiasts) standing. We then joined the railbus, which departed after a short wait, with some forty people standing!

The journey to Wadebridge included calling at all the halts along the way, but was still completed in time to enable us to take a quick look around at the station before rejoining the railbus for the return trip, which began at about 5.10 p.m. This was, I believe, an empty coaching stock working, and we ran non-stop to the Bodmin North side of the exchange platform at Boscarne with about a dozen or so enthusiasts on board. At that point we then waited – as darkness fell – until presently diesel locomotive D6309 arrived from Padstow with a train bound for Bodmin General Station, whereupon a few passengers changed to our railbus and we set off once more with a fair, but not crowded, load at 5.53 p.m.

Apart from a brief stop at Dunmere Halt, which produced no passengers, there were no further delays and we climbed to Bodmin North Station forming what was almost certainly the final *through* passenger working from Wadebridge along the original railway.

At the terminus the passengers detrained while others already waiting on the platform got on board and the final passenger train from Bodmin North after nearly 133 years departed fifteen minutes

Bodmin North Station on 13th January 1967, with the 4-wheel railbus No. 79977 stood alongside the platform.

A view of the two exchange platforms at Boscarne, as seen from the train leaving for Bodmin General Station on 13th January 1967.

late at 6.5 p.m., slipping quietly out of the platform with no ceremony or detonators, just a single blast on the horn of the railbus as she passed the end of the platform. In all about a dozen people saw her go, adorned with a wreath on her front which had been placed there by members of the Launceston Railway Circle.

The passenger trains on the Bodmin Road to Bodmin General and Wadebridge route were also withdrawn on this same day, but the clay trains continued to run from Wenford Bridge, latterly hauled by class '08' diesel-electric shunting locomotives, up until the summer of 1983.

Today the route from Wenford Bridge to Wadebridge and Bodmin is a pedestrian and cycle route, the 'Camel Trail', but the ex-GWR line from Bodmin Road (now Bodmin Parkway) is operated by the Bodmin & Wenford Railway Company as a tourist line. Trains run to Bodmin General Station and down to Boscarne, where a modern platform and run-round loop have been built.

There are ideas of one day extending the line to the outskirts of Wadebridge, so the Bodmin and Wadebridge Railway may, perhaps, be reborn, at least in part. Meanwhile, there is some consolation in the fact that three locomotives associated with the railway have been taken into preservation: 2–4–0 Beattie well tank locomotive No. 30587 is part of the National Collection and from time to time visits various heritage railways; sister locomotive No. 30585 is based at the Buckinghamshire Railway Centre at Quainton Road Station near Aylesbury; and, finally, 0–6–0PT No. 1369 is in the care of the South Devon Railway and is based at Buckfastleigh Station when not visiting other railways.

3. THE BRIXHAM BRANCH

In the second half of the 1930s a school friend and I spent many happy Saturday mornings travelling on our local railways, commencing the journeys from Torre Station on the Kingswear line.

One chosen destination was Brixham, and after purchasing our day return child's tickets (the cost was 7d. – 3p) we would board a 'down' train which took us via Torquay and Paignton stations to Goodrington Sands Halt and then up the long climb to Churston Station.

Alighting here, we would walk back along the 'down' platform past the main station buildings to a short bay platform, with its own waiting shelter; this was at the northern end of the station and where the Brixham train stood ready for yet another journey along the branch.

The bay platform at Churston Station, showing 0–4–2T No. 1466 (formerly No. 4866) and non-corridor coach No. 7392 waiting to provide the next service to Brixham, 16th April 1960.

The locomotive would be a 2–4–0T of the '35xx' class, whilst the passengers were accommodated in one, or sometimes two, auto saloons.

This then was the 'Brixham Whippet', so-called by our fellow

THE BRIXHAM BRANCH

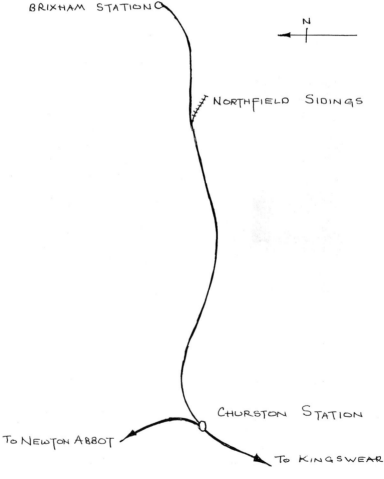

schoolmates from Brixham who attended Torquay Grammar School and used the train regularly.

When departure time came the little train would pull out from the platform, pass under the main Paignton to Brixham and Kingswear road and round a long curve to the east, passing Churston goods yard along the way.

The branch line seen curving away to the east just beyond Churston Station, as 0–4–2T No. 1466 and auto saloon No. 222 arrive with the 4.30 p.m. service from Brixham on 10th May 1952.

Still following an easterly course, the train would then pass through cuttings and proceed along an embankment as it ran near Churston Ferrers village before continuing through open fields to reach the outskirts of Brixham.

Finally, quite a tight curve to the north-east would bring the short journey to a close at Brixham Station (2 miles 1 chain), set around 200 feet above the centre of the town in the valley below. The journey time would normally have been just seven minutes!

Apart from being on a curve, the approach to the terminus was also on a down gradient and the working timetable specified that all 'down' trains must stop at the 'home' signal before 'being steadily drawn' to the platform; as the buffer stops were set high above the steep road leading down to the quays, this seemed a necessary safeguard. (A similar restriction was also in force for 'up' trains on the approach to Churston Station.)

The platform at Brixham was on the left-hand side of the train as it came to rest, and, in addition to the usual station building, a second structure near the end of the platform dealt with the considerable fish traffic from the town's fleet of fishing boats. Milepost 227 stood on the platform, and a neat signal box controlled the signalling and also the pointwork for the run-round loop and the several sidings in the goods yard.

Having arrived at our destination, we would leave the station and descend a flight of stone steps in order to reach the road which passed under the railway. We would then follow it down to the town and harbourside quays, where there was always something of interest to be seen, including the statue of William of Orange – very often with a seagull standing rather impudently on his head! If finances permitted we would indulge in an ice cream before beginning the long climb back to the station in order to catch our train for the return journey.

One such occasion proved to be special, as at the station the engine driver, who was taking a break on a station seat, asked whether we two schoolboys could spell. We said we could, and he stated his test word (I believe it was 'eighth'), promising a reward if we were successful. We managed it correctly and were then allowed to stand with him in the driving compartment of the auto saloon as we returned to Churston, with the locomotive propelling the train. That was a red-letter day indeed!

Unfortunately, I did not record details of the trains on these early trips, but soon afterwards carried a notebook in my pocket and duly wrote down that the Brixham train on 13th May 1940 was formed with 2–4–0T No. 3587 hauling two auto saloons, Nos. 104 and 160.

These rather elderly locomotives continued to be used on the line up until 1943, as I noted No. 3581 with auto saloon No. 167 on 24th May 1940, then No. 3582 with auto saloon No. 160 and a fish van on 31st October 1942 and, finally, No. 3587 with auto saloon No. 167 on 13th May 1943. However, later in 1943 I found that the '48xx' class 0–4–2T locomotives had taken over, my first sighting being of No. 4827, with auto saloons Nos. 160 and 167, on 28th

Two studies of Brixham Station:–
Above: Looking towards Churston, 29th September 1951.

Below: Looking towards the stop blocks, 11th May 1963.

August. From that time forward there were only two occasions on which I saw the trains hauled by a locomotive of another type, both of these being 0–6–0PT locomotives – No. 5412 on 30th July 1949 and No. 7427 on 29th September 1951. Several members of the '48xx' class were in use, obviously being alternated with duties on the other local branch lines, as I recorded Nos. 4827 – 4839 – 4852 – 4866 – 4870 and, on 14th January 1961, No. 1471 (formerly 4871), which was my last steam-hauled entry. Between 1952 and 1960 the auto saloon most frequently seen was No. 222, this being

Auto saloon No. 222 in the branch bay at Churston Station, seen here coupled to 0–4–2T No. 1427 on 10th May 1952.

of later construction than Nos. 160 and 167 which were in use on the branch train in earlier years.

0756	2nd- SINGLE SINGLE -2nd	0756
	Churston to	
	Churston Brixham Churston Brixham	
	BRIXHAM	
	(W) 7d. Fare 7d. (W)	
	For conditions see over For conditions see over	

By the time of my next visit on 10th June 1961 the diesel era had arrived, the train being the single-car diesel unit 55019. On that day a return trip to Brixham enabled me to see the route from a new viewpoint, as I occupied the rear seat and was able to look back along the track.

The diesel units obviously reduced running costs but did very little to increase passenger numbers, as I found on 25th February 1963 when I made a return trip from Brixham to Churston. The day return fare was 1/– (5p) and the train was single-car diesel unit

55014. After noting diesel locomotive D6327 on shunting duties in one of the sidings, I found myself to be the only passenger on the train, so occupied the front seat as we left at 10.53 a.m. We reached Churston in six minutes, and I was able to retain my seat for the return trip, which again took only six minutes. Not bad value for 5p!

A view of Churston Station on 25th February 1963 as single-car diesel unit 55014 stands in the branch bay and a train from Kingswear pauses at the 'up' platform.

A feature of the line which had not existed when I made my first journeys was a fan of sidings on the right-hand (south) side about half a mile outside Brixham. These were Northfield sidings, laid down sometime in 1940 for the Air Ministry as a wartime installation, and well fenced around in the interests of security.

By April 1963 the line was on the brink of closure, so on the 15th of that month my family and I set off in our car for Dartmouth, where we crossed on the ferry to Kingswear Station. After purchasing day return tickets to Brixham (the fare was 2/8d. – 13p), we then caught the Newton Abbot train to Churston, where we alighted and crossed the footbridge to the branch platform. The branch train was a two-car DMU set, vehicles 51327 and 51312, and when it pulled out at 12.40 p.m. we soon discovered that we were the only passengers. Later, we returned on the 3.15 p.m. service, sitting behind the driver, and again were the only passengers. This was Easter Monday Bank Holiday so it was obvious that the branch, which had served the town since 1868, was now of very little local importance.

Less than a month later, on Saturday, 11th May, the final trains were due to run, the line being scheduled for closure to all traffic on the following Monday. Being fully aware of this, my family and I travelled to Churston Station on that Saturday afternoon in time to see the 3.22 p.m. train arrive from Brixham, which was a three-car DMU set composed of vehicles 51139 – 59033 – 51152. However, the only indication of the line's imminent closure displayed on the train was a small, roughly made notice in each of the two driver's cabs, which read 'Last train' and 'Last day for this branch' respectively.

Later, we saw the train from several other viewpoints as it shuttled up and down the line during the course of the afternoon,

Last day activity as the three-car DMU set passes through open countryside during one of its journeys from Churston to Brixham. Note the small closure notice in the driver's cab.

carrying only a small number of passengers, a proportion of whom were obviously railway enthusiasts. Having done that, we returned to Churston Station just before 5.30 p.m., where we witnessed the arrival of the three-car unit at 5.34 p.m., once again with only a moderate number of passengers. We then joined the train, which presently received more passengers who had alighted from a Kingswear-bound train, but when departure time arrived at 5.45 p.m. the coaches were still not more than half full.

We pulled out with no ceremony, not even a 'toot' on the diesel's horn, and ran through to Brixham in six minutes, arriving to the sound of a single detonator.

A small crowd here waited to join the train and, as most of the passengers remained in their seats, the return journey commenced with the train quite well filled.

We left at 5.59 p.m., again with no ceremony or 'toot' on the horn, and, apart from a few people watching from lineside houses, most of Brixham ignored its last train.

Therefore many people must have wondered what was happening when, after we had travelled a few yards, a detonator suddenly exploded. It was followed by another, then more in quick succession and, finally, a thunderous fusillade, leaving a cloud of blue smoke and thirty-six empty detonator cases on the rails.

The rest of the journey passed without incident, the unit halting at the 'home' signal at Churston before drawing into the branch platform at 6.6 p.m.; here just two people were waiting to greet the train. The passengers then alighted and dispersed to the other platforms to await a connecting train or to their waiting cars as the unit reversed out of the bay at 6.12 p.m. It would presently have crossed to the 'up' side of the station and departed to Newton Abbot after having been the final train along a branch line which had closed just five years short of its centenary.

Today the station at Churston forms part of the Paignton & Dartmouth Steam Railway, a mainly tourist line which is operated for some eight months of each year. It is kept in excellent condition and a large maintenance depôt has been erected at the rear of the 'up' platform. Elsewhere, the bay is used for storing rolling stock, and the former goods yard is now the site of a turntable.

At Brixham new housing estates now cover the final three-quarters of a mile of the course and the station area, whilst the 'Brixham Whippet' has, sadly, become just a memory.

*****

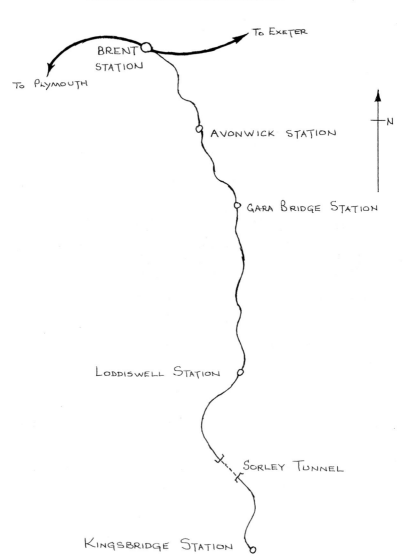

THE KINGSBRIDGE BRANCH

To Exeter

BRENT STATION

To Plymouth

N

AVONWICK STATION

GARA BRIDGE STATION

LODDISWELL STATION

SORLEY TUNNEL

KINGSBRIDGE STATION

NOT TO SCALE

4. THE KINGSBRIDGE BRANCH

The nameboard at Brent Station.

One of the places in Devon which the main line from Paddington to Penzance passes through is the small town of South Brent, on the southern edge of Dartmoor. Here, for many years, there was a busy station – always known simply as Brent – which not only catered for the main line trains, but also served as a junction for a branch line to the town of Kingsbridge, set in the area known as the South Hams.

This line was a comparatively late addition to the railway map, not being opened until 1893 and even then not reaching its original goal, which was the town of Salcombe – some 5 miles beyond Kingsbridge.

My first brief glimpse of the branch train was from a passing main line train on 31st December 1936, when 2–6–2T No. 4571 was

59

standing at the branch platform at Brent attached to two coaches. Then, in April of the following year, as part of a '7 Day Runabout' ticket, a friend and I actually travelled over the line to Kingsbridge and back, although details of the train have, unfortunately, long been forgotten.

Ten years later, whilst on leave from the Army in 1947, I renewed my acquaintance with the line on 6th March, travelling up from Kingsbridge to Brent as part of a circular trip from my home in Torquay. The train consisted of two coaches hauled by 2–6–2T No. 4587 and, at Gara Bridge Station, it crossed 2–6–2T No. 5505 in charge of a goods train.

In 1954 I moved to Plympton, and thereafter was able to visit the line more frequently, the next occasion being on 19th June of that year, when 2–6–2Ts Nos. 5557 and 5539 were working the trains. Two subsequent visits during the following April, however, revealed changes, as on the 7th the branch train was being hauled by BR standard class 3 2–6–2T No. 82033, while six days later sister locomotive No. 82031 was seen carrying out similar duties. This situation, though, was to be very short-lived; these newly introduced locomotives did not prove popular in the area (I also remember seeing them on the Moretonhampstead branch) and by 1st September of the same year the '45xx' class 2–6–2Ts were back, one of them being No. 5558.

At this point in time I had still not had an opportunity to examine the branch in any great detail, but eventually set out to fulfil that wish on 21st April 1956. On that day my wife and I travelled to Brent Station, purchased day return tickets to Kingsbridge at a cost of 3/– (15p) each and then climbed aboard the branch train, which was waiting in its usual place on the southern side of the 'down' platform; it consisted of 2–6–2T No. 5533 with a van and non-corridor coaches Nos. 6279 and 6285, which I think made up, in GWR parlance, a 'B' set. (I never saw an auto train on the branch, and, except as already mentioned, it appeared for many years to rely mainly on the '45xx' class locomotives.)

After receiving the 'right away' at 3.15 p.m., we departed in the 'up' direction, passing under an overbridge and diverging from the main line to run through a cutting in a south-easterly direction before going under the A38 main road. A long curve to the south followed, which took us on falling gradients into the valley of the River Avon near the small village of Avonwick. At that point we

A general view of Brent Station, with the branch platform left centre, 21st April 1956.

The branch line diverging to the right just beyond Brent Station, photographed as a 'down' main line goods train comes into view on 24th September 1955.

61

then began to follow the course of the river southwards, presently passing under the A385 road and reaching our first stopping point, Avonwick Station (2 miles 43 chains); this was situated about half a mile beyond the village that it purported to serve and consisted of a single platform on the left-hand side of the line with very neat, stone buildings. It also had a loop siding, again situated on the left-hand side of the line, complete with a cattle dock.

Avonwick Station, 24th September 1955.

On resuming the journey, the train continued to follow the course of the river, which was crossed no less than four times over the next 3 miles as it meandered down what was an attractive, partly wooded valley. Having done so, the train then also crossed the road from Modbury to Halwell on the level and entered Gara Bridge Station (5 miles 47 chains). Here, the main station buildings were once again situated on the left-hand side of the line, where there was also a loop siding used as a stabling point for camping coaches. Unlike Avonwick Station, however, there were 'up' and 'down' platforms here, a long passing loop so that two trains could cross one another and quite a sizeable signal box, which stood by the level crossing, just beyond the northern end of the 'up' platform.

There was no 'up' train due to cross our train on this journey, so we were given the 'right away' almost immediately and set off down the valley once more, subsequently crossing the river on three more occasions before reaching Topsham Crossing (7 miles 5 chains). This was not a stopping point, just a gated crossing over a

Two views of Gara Bridge Station:–
Above: Looking towards Kingsbridge on 14th September 1963.

Below: Looking towards Brent on 30th May 1955.

minor road deep in the valley with a gatesman's hut and ground frame. (An intriguing feature noted as we ran past was a milk churn standing by the ground frame, and we wondered if it had been brought by the branch goods train in order to provide a water supply to the gatesman at this densely wooded and isolated spot.)

Topsham Crossing, 14th September 1963.

Beyond the level crossing, the train continued down the valley and went on to cross the river in three more places – making it ten in all – until arriving at Loddiswell Station. Situated at 8 miles 72 chains from our starting point, this was very similar to Avonwick, having a single platform on the left-hand side with neat, stone station buildings and a loop siding (in which a camping coach was sited). In addition, there was a gradient post at the southern end of the station site, which indicated that a climb of 1 in 50 lay ahead of our locomotive, and soon No. 5533's exhaust note sounded much more purposeful as she drew out of the station to commence the steep ascent.

The river now fell away below us on the right-hand side and then turned sharply westwards on its way to the estuary at Bantham. Meanwhile, we climbed in a long curve to reach Sorley tunnel (625 yards), emerging at the other end to run down an equally severe gradient on the way to reaching the branch terminus at Kingsbridge (12 miles 35 chains). Sited on the western

Loddiswell Station, looking towards Kingsbridge on 30th May 1955. Note the camping coach to the left of the picture.

side of the town, this was not far from the quay and the lower end of the main street. The platform was set on a curve on the right-hand side, just beyond a large signal box, and, once again, the main station buildings were of a neat design, but bigger than the

The approach to Kingsbridge Station, with the engine shed visible to the right, immediately beyond the water tower, 21st April 1956.

The northern end of Kingsbridge Station, 14th September 1963.

others which we had passed along the route. A small engine shed stood near the platform, and there was a quite extensive goods yard with a goods shed, a short carriage shed and various other structures, including a cattle dock.

After we had alighted, at 3.45 p.m., we walked down to the quay and around the town, later returning to the station in time to see the arrival of the late afternoon service from Brent. Once the passengers had disembarked, we also saw the locomotive (No. 5533 again) run around its train, which we presently boarded and which now consisted only of a van and a single coach, No. 6285.

There was only a brief delay before the return working commenced and, with such a light load, our locomotive had no difficulty in surmounting the gradients as we ran through to Brent, where we completed the journey after stopping only at Gara Bridge. Thus ended a very pleasant trip and one during which it had been encouraging to see that the stations at Gara Bridge and Kingsbridge had recently been repainted.

In the course of the next few years my family and I made several visits to the branch and on each occasion the trains were still being hauled by the '45xx' class locomotives, including Nos. 4561 – 5533 – 5558 and 5573. There was just one exception to this, as on 16th May 1959 we saw a train which arrived at Gara Bridge from Brent

One of the '45xx' class locomotives, No. 4561, entering Gara Bridge Station with a train to Kingsbridge on 21st March 1961.

at 12.38 p.m. being crossed by a train from Kingsbridge headed by an 0–6–0PT, No. 9633. It was, incidentally, hauling two coaches, three vans and a guard's van – a typical 'mixed' branch train.

Twelve months later, on 28th May 1960, a day return trip from Brent to Kingsbridge (now at a cost of 3/9d. – 19p) revealed 2–6–2T No. 5558 in charge of a four-coach train. Returning on the 5.40 p.m. service from Kingsbridge, now with only two coaches, the train suddenly slowed near Gara Bridge as the locomotive's cylinder draincocks were used to good effect to clear an unexpected obstruction – four goats had strayed onto the line! In spite of this, however, the journey back to Brent was still completed in twenty-four minutes.

A major change in the branch passenger service took place as from 12th June 1961, when single-car diesel unit trains replaced the steam-hauled ones. My first sighting of the new trains came just over a month later, on 29th July, when single-car diesel unit 55013 was waiting in the branch platform at Brent Station.

At this time, however, it was still possible to see steam-hauled trains on Saturdays, when through coaches from main line trains were worked down the branch to Kingsbridge. For example, on 26th August 1961, whilst single-car diesel unit 55013 was

Single-car diesel unit 55013 approaching Gara Bridge Station from Kingsbridge on 26th August 1961.

2–6–2T No. 5525, hauling three through coaches from Paddington and one non-corridor coach, seen leaving Gara Bridge Station for Kingsbridge on 26th August 1961.

providing the normal branch service and was seen by my family and I arriving at Gara Bridge from Kingsbridge just before 5 p.m., a 'down' train soon appeared headed by 2–6–2T No. 5525; it was hauling three well-filled corridor coaches (the through portion) and one non-corridor coach. On that day there were two camping coaches in the siding here, but we were unable to see whether any of the passengers alighted to take up temporary residence at this very rural location. We did, however, see both trains presently depart, whereupon quietness returned to Gara Bridge once more.

The single-car diesel unit had one very good feature, in that if one could secure the seats immediately behind the driver's compartment it was possible to have a clear view of the track ahead, or to the rear if travelling in the opposite direction. On 16th September 1961 I purchased a single ticket from Kingsbridge to Gara Bridge (the fare was 1/9d. – 9p) and secured the rear seats in single-car diesel unit 55013.

Departure was at 7.30 p.m. and we climbed with the speedometer (visible through the glass partition of the vacant driver's compartment) reading 36 mph as the train approached the tunnel at Sorley. The view whilst threading the tunnel was a

69

different experience, quickly followed by the descent of the gradient leading to Loddiswell Station, where a camping coach was still stationed in the siding. From there, the train continued to Gara Bridge, which was reached at 7.45 p.m., and I alighted and walked to the waiting family car as the evening light faded into the 'dimpsie', as we say here in Devon.

By 1963 it had become evident that the trains would be withdrawn in the near future, so my family and I decided to take a ride over the line on 13th April of that year for what proved to be the penultimate time.

We caught the 12 noon train from Brent, which consisted of single-car diesel unit 55000, and, having secured the rear seats, noticed that at one point along the way the speedometer was seen to read 40 mph. (The top permitted speed over the branch was 35 mph!)

Our arrival at Kingsbridge was nearly two minutes early – I wonder why! – and after a short walk around we returned on the 2.5 p.m. train, this time securing the front seats, which added to the pleasure of the trip and enabled us to enjoy views of the river and the lineside wild daffodils and primroses.

The unwelcome 'Notice of Closure' appeared later that year stating that the line would be closed to all traffic from 16th

Single-car diesel unit 55000 at Kingsbridge Station on 13th April 1963.

September 1963, which meant that the last trains would run on the 14th of that month.

When that day arrived we first of all set off by car to visit the stations along the line, starting at Avonwick Station, where we saw the train just after 12 noon. There was not a large number of passengers on it at that time, but things were to change later in the day and it was fortunate that more vehicles had been provided, in the form of a two-car diesel multiple unit set. (This formation operated all the branch trains that day, and consisted of vehicles 50869 and 50922, together with single-car diesel unit 55001, making a three-car train.)

The last-day train, seen here leaving Avonwick Station for Kingsbridge just after 12 noon.

After moving on to Gara Bridge Station, we saw the train again at around 2.30 p.m., on its way to Brent, and, after checking with the signalman that it would not return until after 5 p.m., we continued, in turn, to Topsham Crossing, Loddiswell Station and Kingsbridge Station. Having taken some photographs and spent some time in Kingsbridge, we then drove to Brent and joined the small crowd on the station to await the arrival of the train.

It drew into the platform at 6.30 p.m. and, in contrast to earlier in the day, was full to overflowing with many passengers standing. Some of these alighted, and we boarded the front coach as the train

71

once again filled to capacity before departing at 6.46 p.m., with the leading coach setting off about a dozen detonators as we turned onto the branch.

Down at Avonwick about five people were standing on the platform, and here one lady alighted, her final journey on the branch completed. A five-minute run commencing at 6.52 p.m. then brought us to Gara Bridge, where, once again, some five people awaited us. From there, following a stop of only one minute, we continued to Loddiswell and received a similar greeting before pulling out of the station at 7.5 p.m. and commencing the steep climb to Sorley tunnel, which was made without undue effort; after that, the units ran easily down the gradients to Kingsbridge Station, where we arrived at 7.13 p.m. to be greeted by another small crowd of waiting people.

I alighted from our coach and walked to the rear (now to be the front) of the train, where a wreath was being attached to the buffer beam. After a few minutes, the passengers then rejoined the train and, in spite of a false start, we commenced the final journey up the line at 7.30 p.m., as dusk began to fall.

At Loddiswell one or two detrained to join a handful of people already standing on the platform there, then we were away again at 7.38 p.m., presently passing Topsham Crossing, where the peace of the valley was shattered by a volley of eight detonators.

The evening mist was now gathering like cotton wool in the lineside fields as we made our way to Gara Bridge, arriving there at 7.45 p.m. to find about a dozen people waiting to see us pass. A slight delay ensued as we waited while more detonators were laid, and these exploded in an eight-fold salute, together with 'toots' from the unit's horn, as we left at 7.48 p.m.

A group of people waiting beside the line near Bickham Bridge received another 'toot' and then we were running into Avonwick Station at 7.53 p.m., where some passengers detrained.

A memory here is of looking ahead out of a window as we entered the cutting near Avonwick village and seeing the black silhouette of the moors in the gathering darkness, surmounted by a beautiful pink sunset.

Figuratively speaking, the sun was also setting on the little trains to Kingsbridge as we approached Brent Station a few minutes later to the sound of more exploding detonators. Then, after we had drawn to a halt alongside the branch platform at 8.0 p.m., the train emptied, the passengers drifted away and we walked back to our car knowing that we had lost yet another friendly branch line.

In the months following closure all the track was lifted, and in October 1964 the station at Brent was closed to passenger traffic, breaking the final link with the trains to Kingsbridge.

Today the site of the track at Brent Station where the branch trains stood is now part of a car park, whilst part of the track bed just outside the town has long since been bisected by the re-routed A38 main road.

The stations at Avonwick, Gara Bridge and Loddiswell have been converted to dwellings, whilst Sorley tunnel has become part of a tourist complex, and the station area at Kingsbridge now contains an industrial site. However, it is still possible to explore part of the line in the Avon valley, as a public footpath extends from outside the site of Loddiswell Station to the former Topsham Crossing, taking in part of the track bed, and is marked on the 1:25000 scale Ordnance Survey map as 'Woodland Walks'.

*****

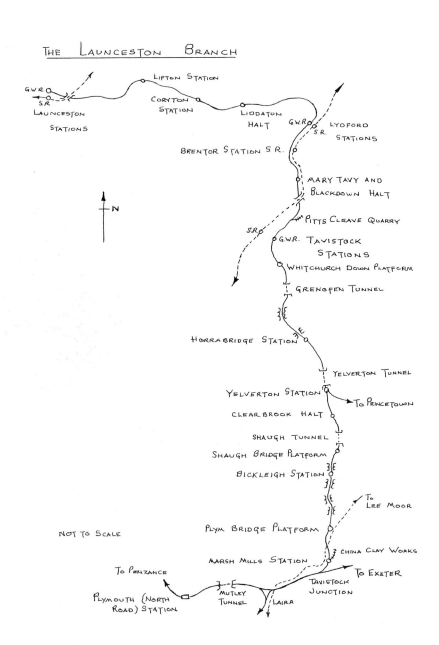

5. THE LAUNCESTON BRANCH

The Launceston branch, with a length of over 30 miles, was one of the longest branch lines in the West Country, passing, as it did, through a large part of the south-western corner of Devon before crossing into Cornwall.

My first experience of the line came in August 1934 during a family holiday at Launceston, when we purchased day return tickets to Lydford, but I was too young to record the details of the trains. (As long as I was able to ride on a train hauled by a steam locomotive I was quite happy. I still feel that way today!)

A little over two years later, on 31st December 1936, my paternal grandfather took me on my first visit to the Princetown branch, and this entailed travelling over another part of the Launceston branch – from Plymouth to Yelverton, and back.

The day began by joining a train from our 'home' station of Torre and travelling via Newton Abbot to Plymouth, where we alighted at Mutley Station, which was still in use at that time. Here we booked our return tickets to Princetown and awaited the 10.46 a.m. train to Yelverton. (I still have my child's ticket numbered 5878, cut diagonally in half by the booking clerk.)

The train, made up of 0–6–0PT No. 6419 hauling two auto saloons, presently arrived from North Road Station and we then departed through Mutley tunnel, ran down past Laira engine sheds, went over the level crossing with the Lee Moor Tramway and, with the Plym estuary on our right, soon reached Tavistock Junction. Here our train curved to the north before stopping at the 'down' platform of Marsh Mills Station, situated a mere 18 chains from the junction. Trains were able to cross here, and sidings on the 'up' side served a stone crushing plant, whilst a steeply graded line led to the Dartmoor China Clay Co.'s processing works, again on the 'up' side.

After restarting from the station, we entered the narrowing valley of the River Plym and ran in close proximity to the rails of

Marsh Mills Station, looking northwards on 4th June 1955.

the 4 feet 6 inches gauge Lee Moor Tramway for quite some distance, unfortunately without seeing any sign of a horse-drawn train of wagons. Initially, the tramway was on our left-hand (western) side, but in just under a mile from Marsh Mills Station it swopped sides by making a diagonal crossing on the level with the GWR line at Lee Moor Crossing; this was protected in both directions by 'home' and 'distant' signals operated from an adjoining signal box.

Beyond the level crossing our train was soon approaching Plym Bridge Platform (1 mile 39 chains), which was an unstaffed 'halt' consisting of a single wooden platform with a small shelter on the right-hand side of the line. From here, a path led down to the nearby road and the ancient bridge after which the platform was named, and it was possible to see the bridge by which the Lee Moor Tramway crossed the same road as it commenced its ascent of the long Cann Wood incline.

Our locomotive now faced an almost unbroken climb of nearly 6 miles, including lengthy stretches where the ruling gradient was as steep as 1 in 60, or even 1 in 58. Consequently, it was hardly surprising that the exhaust note of the little pannier tank deepened as we resumed the journey, which immediately entailed the crossing of two bridges. Of these, the first carried the line over the nearby road, whilst the second took us over the long-disused Cann

Quarry line (and canal) – just beyond the point where it formerly branched off the Lee Moor Tramway.

Over the course of the next half-mile or so we passed through an area of picturesque woodland and could see the route of the former Cann Quarry line (and its attendant canal) down below us to our left, running in close proximity to the River Plym. But then, after going under a stone accommodation bridge, we finally crossed the river by means of the Cann viaduct, which was constructed of blue Staffordshire brick and had a maximum height of 63 feet. One of several such structures on this line, the viaduct also passed over the route of the earlier railway (and canal), and from it could be glimpsed the grim face of the disused Cann Quarry.

Beyond this point the pleasant wooded scenery continued for almost two more miles, during the course of which our train first of all encountered Riverford viaduct, standing at a maximum height of 97 feet, and then the even higher (125 feet) Bickleigh viaduct. After that, the woodland began to recede, and soon the exhaust of our locomotive was reverberating against the sides of quite a deep cutting as we neared Bickleigh Station (4 miles 9 chains).

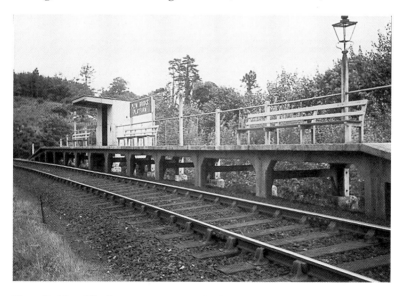

Plym Bridge Platform, as seen on 25th September 1954. By then the original wooden platform had been replaced by a somewhat ugly concrete structure.

The cutting immediately to the south of Bickleigh Station, with 0–6–0PT No. 6414 seen propelling auto saloon No. 51 on an ECS (empty coaching stock) working, 7th April 1956.

As we drew into the station it could be seen that passing facilities were provided here and that there were two platforms, the main station buildings being sited on the 'down' platform, whilst a signal box and waiting room stood on the 'up' side. Set high on a hillside, and situated about half a mile from the village that it purported to serve, the station also had a goods siding at the southern end of the 'down' side and a water crane at the northern end. In addition, a prominent feature was a substantial house for the stationmaster, which stood adjacent to the 'down' platform.

On resuming the journey, our train soon reached the nearby

Bickleigh Station, looking towards Yelverton on 13th January 1962.

Ham Green viaduct (maximum height 91 feet) and then ran along the shoulder of a hill for well over half a mile before arriving at Shaugh Bridge Platform (4 miles 79 chains). Built on a curve, the single platform was placed on the right-hand side of the line and had a small, pagoda waiting shelter. From here, also to the right, we could see the rocky outcrop of the Dewerstone above the confluence of the rivers Plym and Meavy.

Shaugh Bridge Platform, 7th April 1956.

Almost at once after leaving Shaugh Bridge Platform our train entered Shaugh tunnel (308 yards in length) and emerged into the valley of the Meavy, where it again proceeded to run along the shoulder of a hill for some considerable distance. We then stopped briefly at Clearbrook Halt (6 miles 25 chains), which had a single platform and waiting shelter on the left-hand side of the line, and from there went on to complete our outward journey along the branch at Yelverton Station (7 miles 37 chains).

At Yelverton we alighted on the 'down' platform. Then, after watching the train depart and disappear into Yelverton tunnel, we crossed the footbridge in order to reach the 'up' platform, which had a curved extension at its northern end for passengers travelling on the Princetown branch. Meanwhile, as we looked around, it was apparent that the station itself was quite an imposing affair, incorporating not only the 'up' and 'down' platforms and footbridge, but also a number of other features that included a passing loop, a goods siding, a signal box and a water crane. The main station building, constructed of vertical timber planking under a hipped

Clearbrook Halt, 7th April 1956.

Yelverton Station, looking towards Tavistock on 10th January 1959.

roof, was situated on the 'down' platform immediately to the north of a pagoda shelter, and there was a many-sided building of similar construction directly opposite, on the 'up' platform, for passengers awaiting trains going in the Plymouth and Princetown directions. On that day, however, we had no need to use this latter facility as the Princetown train was already waiting for us. (Our subsequent journey to Princetown and back was somewhat spoiled by bad weather, but we eventually returned home at the end of our day's excursion feeling that it had, nevertheless, been well worthwhile.)

Having now covered parts of the Launceston line, it was my firm intention to complete the experience and travel through to its terminus, but, as events transpired, it was to be nearly thirteen years before my ambition was realised. Then, at long last, on 28th April 1949, my parents and I were able to set off from Torre Station, travel via Newton Abbot to Plymouth and join the 3.10 p.m. Launceston-bound train at North Road Station. The train itself was made up of three coaches hauled by 2–6–2T No. 5540 and, because of my earlier excursion to Princetown, followed by another in July 1945, the journey as far as Yelverton was reasonably familiar. It did, however, include the crossing of an 'up' train at Bickleigh, which consisted of 2–6–2T No. 4524 with two coaches and two milk tankers, the latter almost certainly from the factory at Lifton.

On arriving at Yelverton, it was interesting to reflect that our train, which had been only a few feet above sea level as it ran beside the Plym estuary, had now reached an altitude of over 500 feet.

Following a brief lull, the journey resumed with our train entering the 641-yard-long Yelverton tunnel. Then, after emerging on the northern outskirts of the village, we continued on what had now become a falling gradient for just over a mile until crossing the A386 main road between Yelverton and Tavistock by means of a girder bridge and arriving at our next stopping point. This was Horrabridge Station (8 miles 77 chains), where, once again, passing facilities were provided and there were 'up' and 'down' platforms, the main station building being on the former and standing next to a signal box. The station also boasted a number of other structures, amongst which was an open-fronted waiting shelter on the 'down' platform, a water tower, two water cranes and, just beyond the northern end of the 'up' platform, quite a large goods shed.

From here the village of Horrabridge lay below us on the

Horrabridge Station, 25th November 1961.

Trains crossing at Horrabridge Station. In this photograph, taken on 30th May 1959, 2–6–2T No. 4592 is seen arriving with a train to Launceston, while 2–6–2T No. 5531 is waiting with a train to Plymouth.

right-hand side of the train, and we enjoyed the view from the carriage window as we continued on a falling gradient, crossing Magpie viaduct (maximum height 62 feet) and then the great Walkham (or Grenofen) viaduct that passed over the river after which it was named at a maximum height of 132 feet.

Now followed a relatively short stretch of line on a rising gradient as our locomotive took us up into Grenofen tunnel (374 yards long), after which the downgrade resumed as we neared Whitchurch Down Platform (11 miles 65 chains). A single platform with a waiting shelter on the right-hand side of the line served passengers here, and, after receiving the 'right away' from our guard, it took only a few more minutes to reach Tavistock.

Whitchurch Down Platform, 8th December 1956.

Situated at 12 miles 71 chains from Tavistock Junction, and conveniently placed near the centre of the town that it served, the station here was by far the busiest and most important on the branch. It was also distinguished by being the only one amongst them to feature an overall roof, as well as by having easily the most complex and comprehensive track layout, which incorporated a long passing loop and a vast array of sidings. The station buildings, too, were substantial, the main one being sited on the 'up' platform, just to the north of the signal box, and amongst the many other facilities was an extensive, fully equipped goods yard, which was set on the 'down' side. On the way into the station, incidentally, I had noticed an 'up' train preparing to leave for Plymouth, which consisted of a '45xx' class 2–6–2T and two coaches.

Having reached Tavistock, we had now completed the route of the original line – the South Devon & Tavistock Railway, which had been opened in 1859 – and were waiting for our locomotive's water tanks to be replenished before setting off on the remainder of our journey. This, of course, would be on the line which had been opened in 1865 as the Launceston & South Devon Railway, and at 4 p.m. we were finally on our way with a whistle being heard from No. 5540 as she pulled out to face what would soon become an almost unbroken climb of around 6 miles.

Tavistock (GWR) Station, looking towards Launceston on 3rd October 1960.

On reaching the north-eastern outskirts of the town, we crossed the River Tavy and ran beside it for some distance, passing Kelly College on our left and then the sidings and works of Pitts Cleave Quarry on our right. After that, though, the line began to swing around to the north and, instead of continuing alongside the River Tavy, we entered the valley of one of its tributaries, the River Burn. Almost coincidentally, the double track of the Southern main line between Plymouth and Exeter appeared on our left-hand side, while shortly afterwards our train passed beneath two overbridges in relatively quick succession. Of these, the first took us under the

A386 main road between Tavistock and Okehampton, whilst the second carried the Southern main line over our branch line, after which the two soon started to run parallel to one another as they continued up the valley.

Nearly a mile further on we stopped at Mary Tavy and Blackdown Halt (16 miles 23 chains), originally a station provided with passing facilities which had been removed many years before our visit. Only the 'up' platform remained in use, but a stone-built waiting shelter was still standing on the site of the former 'down' platform, albeit totally isolated. (There was no stopping point on the main line at this spot; instead, there was a separate station further up the valley that served the village of North Brentor.)

Mary Tavy and Blackdown Halt, 23rd June 1956. Note the long-disused and overgrown 'down' platform on the left-hand side of the track.

The double track Southern main line and the single track branch continued to run side by side until we reached Lydford Station (19 miles 43 chains), which marked the end of the adverse gradient from Tavistock and was the highest point on the line at 650 feet above sea level. Although not obvious to the casual observer, especially as the entire site was worked from one (joint) signal box, there were actually two stations here existing side by side. The arrangements were such that the branch 'down' platform was on the western side, whilst 'up' trains on the branch used one side (the western) of a central island platform, the other side of which was for 'up' main line trains. Then, completing the layout, there was a third platform on the eastern side of the site for 'down' main line trains.

2–6–2T No. 5551 passing Brentor Station (SR) whilst in charge of the 11.30 a.m. service from Tavistock on 23rd June 1956.

Lydford (GWR) Station, looking towards Launceston on 30th May 1959.

As we drew alongside the 'down' platform a branch goods train was waiting on the 'up' side, hauled by a '45xx' class 2–6–2T with its tanks adorned with a bundle of peasticks! Beyond it, at the northern end of the site, we could also see a large goods shed which, for a few years up until 1892 (when the Launceston branch was converted from Brunel's 7 feet $0^1/4$ inch gauge), had been used for the transfer of loads between standard- and broad-gauge wagons.

Liddaton Halt, 23rd June 1956.

Our train departed again at 4.14 p.m., leaving the Southern line to continue climbing to its summit near Aliceford whilst we passed the Manor Hotel on our left and curved to run in a westerly direction. Now in the wooded valley of the River Lyd, we descended on gradients of 1 in 55 to 57 high above Lydford Gorge and, after almost 3 miles, reached Liddaton Halt (22 miles 35 chains). Here the platform and waiting shelter were of wooden construction, placed on the right-hand side of the line. A small Methodist chapel stood nearby, but the hamlet of Liddaton Green was some half a mile away. Strangely enough, the halt was situated at an almost equal distance from the village of Coryton in an easterly direction as the next station, named Coryton, was to the west.

The train's steep descent continued as we ran down to, and crossed, the river River Lyd before reaching Coryton Station (23 miles 76 chains); this comprised a single platform and station building set on the right-hand side of the line, together with a goods siding.

Coryton Station, 23rd June 1956.

Lifton Station, 30th May 1959.

We had now reached the bottom of the valley, and the gradient eased considerably as the journey continued, sometimes very near the winding river which we recrossed at one point and then crossed a third time as we drew into the station at Lifton (27 miles 14 chains). This was a passing place with two platforms and also sidings serving the adjacent milk factory, situated on the northern side of the station site. The main station building was on the 'up' platform, immediately to the east of a goods shed and opposite a small waiting shelter on the 'down' platform, and there was a signal box just beyond the 'up' platform, at the Lydford end.

Now on the final lap of the journey, No. 5540 restarted her train, first crossing a road on the level and then the river once more prior to following the latter in a sweeping curve for nearly a mile. After that, it was only a short distance before we made yet another crossing of the river, but this was for the final time as we were now less than half a mile away from its confluence with the River Tamar, which was about to become our next companion. However, it was to be a very brief acquaintance, as not long afterwards we also crossed this river, the last mile or so of the line being in Cornwall, in the valley of the River Kensey.

We passed beneath the Southern line between Halwill Junction and Padstow as we approached our destination, terminating at the former GWR station at Launceston (31 miles 64 chains*) at 4.39 p.m. The journey had been a very pleasant one, with scenery ranging from wooded river valleys to moorland hills, and quite remarkably had included running in close proximity to no less than eight different rivers.

Apart from the ex-GWR terminus, there was also a station at Launceston on the Southern line, and this was situated only a short distance away to the south. However, except for the signalling arrangements, which were similar to those at Lydford, the two stations were quite separate from one another. They did, though, have a rail connection between them, which, I believe, had been installed during the Second World War.

At the former GWR station there were two platforms, the main station building being on the longer (northern) one, whilst a small engine shed, water tower, turntable, goods shed and several sidings completed what was a typical branch line terminus.

*This distance (and others previously given) is that from Tavistock Junction – the total distance from Plymouth (North Road) Station was 35 miles 38 chains.

The end of the line! A view of Launceston (GWR) Station looking eastwards towards Lifton on 13th April 1957.

Both stations were at some disadvantage by being situated at the bottom of a steep hill, below the town, but they also served the nearby communities of Newport and St Stephen's, set mostly at the same level in the Kensey valley. In spite of the steep climb involved, we decided to visit the town and the grounds of Launceston Castle, from where we later returned to the station in time to catch the 6.15 p.m. train back to Plymouth. This, in fact, was the return working of our outward trip, and during the course of the journey we crossed a 'down' train at Tavistock consisting of three coaches hauled by 2–6–2T No. 4591. (This locomotive must have been on the branch for a considerable number of years, as I subsequently saw it on numerous occasions up to and including the final day of passenger services.)

Our train eventually reached Plymouth (North Road) Station at 7.55 p.m., and from there we returned via Newton Abbot to our starting point at Torre Station to round off a most enjoyable day.

Apart from a journey as far as Yelverton in order to travel over the Princetown line in 1953, there now ensued another gap in my visits to the branch until a change of circumstances occurred in 1954. In that year, having recently married, I obtained a post in Plympton and moved into a house at Woodford, at the western end of the town, which was within easy walking distance of Marsh Mills Station. Thus, from that time forward, it was possible to visit the line much more frequently.

My wife and I first patronised the branch together on 5th June 1954, when we purchased day return tickets to Lydford (the fare from Marsh Mills Station was 4/6d. – 23p) and boarded the 10.47 a.m. train, which was made up of 2–6–2T No. 5569 and five coaches. On that day, now over fifty years ago, much activity was evident: on the outward journey we crossed 2–6–2T No. 4530 in charge of a freight train at Bickleigh, did the same to 2–6–2T No. 4583 on a three-coach 'up' train at Yelverton, and later saw 0–6–0PT No. 3790 engaged in shunting duties at Horrabridge. We then went on to reach Tavistock at 11.28 a.m. and, after the two rear coaches had been detached, set off again, calling at Mary Tavy and Blackdown Halt before climbing with the great sweep of Blackdown on our right towards Lydford Station, where we eventually arrived at 11.49 a.m.

Almost three pleasant hours were spent hereabouts before we returned to the station to catch the 2.46 p.m. 'up' train. It could be heard coming up the gradient from Lifton, with 2–6–2T No. 5531 in charge of two coaches and a van; after we had boarded, the down-hill section to Tavistock was taken much more easily and we arrived there in time to see a six-coach train (including three ex-SR vehicles) headed by 2–6–2T No 4542; this had terminated here after its journey from Plymouth. After leaving Tavistock at 3.04 p.m., we saw no other trains until Bickleigh, where we crossed 2–6–2T No. 4591 and two coaches. We then ended our day out at Marsh Mills at 3.36 p.m.

The trip had given me an insight into the working of the branch, with no less than six '45xx' class 2–6–2Ts and one 0–6–0PT seen in use on various trains during the day.

A pleasant way to spend a fine summer's evening was to catch the 6.30 p.m. train from Marsh Mills Station, travel as far as Shaugh Bridge Platform (the return fare was 1/2d. – 6p) and walk to the beauty spot of Shaugh Bridge. On the evening of 22nd July 1954 the train of three coaches was headed by 2–6–2T No. 4591, and we alighted at the Platform at 6.44 p.m. with almost three hours to enjoy the scenery before returning to catch the 9.35 p.m. 'up' train. It presently arrived in the gathering dusk, consisting of 0–6–0PT No. 6414 and a single coach, and we took only eleven minutes to coast down to our destination, passing through Plym Bridge Platform non-stop on the way.

A day trip to Yelverton on 30th August 1955, in order to visit the Princetown branch (in its final summer of operation), commenced by joining the 1.55 p.m. train from Marsh Mills Station. It was a surprise to see 0–4–2T No. 1408 appear around the curve from Tavistock Junction (hauling an auto saloon and two ex-LMS coaches), as I had never previously seen one of these locomotives on the branch. However, she took us up to Yelverton with no trouble, and we were able to join the Princetown train without delay.

After a pleasant few hours on the moors, we returned to Yelverton in the evening, and from here 2–6–2T No. 4542 (with four coaches) took us back down to Marsh Mills, where we alighted at 7.16 p.m.

Many other visits were made to the branch during the next few years, including spending some time at Yelverton on 3rd March 1956 in connection with the last day trains on the Princetown line. However, only a selection can be mentioned here, and the first that comes to mind after that melancholy day in March is a journey undertaken on 9th June 1956, when my wife and I joined the 2.17 p.m. train at Marsh Mills Station.

On that day the train consisted of 2–6–2T No. 4590 coupled to auto saloon No. 155, brake third coach No. 5121 and auto saloon No. 157, and this took us as far as Tavistock, the return fare being 2/6d. (12^1/$_2$p). After alighting there, we looked around the town and then returned to the station in order to join the 4.0 p.m. service to Launceston, which was formed by a two-coach train in the charge of 2–6–2T No. 5569 and cost 6/– (30p) for two day return tickets.

Once the journey had commenced we soon reached Mary Tavy and Blackdown Halt, which, by then, was almost derelict, and completed the climb to Lydford, where we crossed 2–6–2T No. 5506 in charge of a freight train. From there, we then continued to Lifton, but in open country beyond the station the train came to a sudden halt: the guard alighted and shut a carriage door which had become ajar, remarking "Everything in our favour's against us". He then climbed aboard once more and Launceston was reached without further incident, but on our arrival we took the connecting spur and stopped at the 'down' platform of the former SR station. (The reason for this apparent anomaly was that the ex-GWR station was no longer used by passenger trains, and the turntable had been removed, although the locomotive shed appeared to be still in use.)

2–6–2T No. 5568 arrives at the 'down' platform of the former SR station at Launceston with a train from Plymouth on 3rd November 1962.

After going for a walk, we made our way back to the station in time to catch the 5.40 p.m. return train, which departed from the former SR 'up' platform and was the same locomotive and coaches that had brought us here. The journey was very pleasant on that summer's evening and, after crossing 2–6–2T No. 5551 and two coaches at Yelverton, we alighted at Marsh Mills at 7.16 p.m., having journeyed for 63 miles at a cost of 5/6d. (27^1/2p) each.

Just over a fortnight later, on another fine summer's evening, my father and I caught the 6.30 p.m. train from Marsh Mills to Yelverton, a two-coach train in the charge of 2–6–2T No. 5567.

After alighting at Yelverton, we walked back across Roborough Down, following part of the course of the old Plymouth & Dartmoor Railway, which still had some of its stone sleepers *in situ*. We then came off the Down and descended to Shaugh Bridge Platform in order to await the arrival of our return train; it presently appeared in the gathering darkness at 9.45 p.m. and consisted of 2–6–2T No. 4590 coupled to auto saloon No. 51. Apart from some railwaymen coming off duty, we were the only passengers that night, and, after we had alighted at Marsh Mills, the locomotive took the single coach around the curve and out of our sight as it joined the main line on its way to Plymouth.

The branch train played a part in our family history on 5th January 1957, when our infant daughter was given her first ride in a train, tucked up cosily in her pram. On that day we joined the 2.13 p.m. service from Marsh Mills to Plymouth (North Road) Station, travelling in the guard's compartment of a two-coach train headed by 2–6–2T No. 4592. Later, we returned on the 5.25 p.m. train and heard no complaints from our daughter!

Passenger numbers on the branch trains were quite dramatically increased in the week of 21st to 28th July 1957, when employees of the local bus company went on strike, several trains seen at Marsh Mills being full to capacity.

On 14th August of the same year an experimental 'Land Cruise' train was operated, whose itinerary included the Launceston branch. At the time my parents were staying with us and I persuaded them to travel on this train, which departed from Plymouth (North Road) Station and ran firstly down the main line towards Penzance as far as Bodmin Road. It then ran up to Bodmin General Station, and from there reversed down to Wadebridge and on to Padstow before making a lengthy stop. After that, the train travelled over the former SR line to Launceston, where it went across the connecting spur to the ex-GWR line and returned via the branch to Plymouth (North Road) Station.

Although I had been unable to go on this trip, I saw the train at Marsh Mills in the evening and recorded that it was made up of 2–6–2Ts Nos. 5551 and 5569, six coaches and a cafeteria car. Later, my parents said that they had enjoyed the ride, but added that the train had only been about half full. (It ran again on 14th August of the following year, but on that occasion – the last as far as I am aware – there were only four coaches and a cafeteria car, the locomotives being 2–6–2Ts Nos. 5567 and 4592, both in lined green livery.)

The Tavistock Goose Fair is held annually in October, and in 1961 the date fell on the 11th of the month. My parents were again staying with us, and decided to visit Tavistock in order to see the festivities, riding in the 10.47 a.m. train from Marsh Mills.

The railway authorities had apparently forgotten the significance of the day, as when the train appeared it consisted of a single auto saloon, packed with passengers, and 2–6–2T No. 5568. This turned out to be a bonus for my parents, because they were permitted to sit on the seats in the driver's compartment and were then able to look back along the track in observation car style. The

WEDNESDAY, AUGUST 14th

Something really new!

AN ALL DAY
"LAND CRUISE"
TO THE
NORTH CORNISH COAST
returning via Launceston and Tavistock

THROUGH MORE THAN 100 MILES OF THE MOST GLORIOUS SCENERY IN DEVON AND CORNWALL

9/6
SECOND CLASS

with a 4 hours' stop in Wadebridge or Padstow and a 1½ hours' stop in Tavistock.

CAFETERIA CAR FACILITIES
YOUR SEAT RESERVED WITHOUT EXTRA CHARGE

TICKETS FOR THE LAND CRUISE must be obtained at the ENQUIRY OFFICE Plymouth (North Road) Station. BOOKINGS WILL COMMENCE AT 9-0 a.m. ON MONDAY, JULY 8th.

Children under Three years of age will be conveyed Free; Three Years and under Fourteen at half-fare.

BOOK EARLY—ACCOMMODATION IS LIMITED

The front page of a leaflet advertising the 'Land Cruise'.

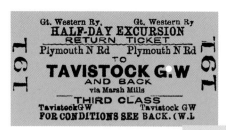

return trip, at 4.30 p.m., was well patronised but not packed out, and consisted of auto saloons Nos. 228 and 244 propelled by 2–6–2T No. 5572.

In January 1962 leaflets appeared in the branch trains giving details of the proposed closure of the line. Headed 'Notice to the Public', the script included a paragraph stating, in effect, that new diesel units being introduced would still not make the line profitable, thereby nullifying any possible suggestion from opponents of the closure.

The trains continued to operate as before, but the line was being run down, the weather adding to the gloom with a very wet day on the bank holiday of 6th August. The 10.47 a.m. train at Marsh Mills, which in earlier years would have been crowded with day trippers, arrived from Plymouth with 0–6–0PT No. 6438 hauling three auto saloons (Nos. 234 – 228 – 230) and converted passenger brake van No. 255, but with under a dozen passengers.

In the following November a sheet was posted at Marsh Mills Station giving notice of the closure of the branch as from 31st December 1962. As a result, and with the prospect of crowds of people giving a carnival atmosphere on the last day trains, we decided to have a final, 'normal' ride to Launceston. The chosen date was 1st December, and, in order to cover the entire length of the branch, we went to Plymouth (North Road) Station and travelled on the 10.40 a.m. train, which consisted of 2–6–2T No. 5564 and two corridor coaches, one of GWR origin and one of LMSR origin.

On the way we crossed 2–6–2T No. 4574 in charge of a freight train at Marsh Mills and also 2–6–2T No. 5569 on a two-coach train at Horrabridge, then later, on arriving at Launceston at 12.15 p.m., we saw 2–6–2T No. 4591 engaged in shunting duties in the ex-GWR station.

We did not go up into the town on this occasion. Instead, we decided to go back home on the 12.40 p.m. train, which was, of course, the return working of our outward one. We then went on to cross just one more train, which consisted of 0–6–0PT No. 6400 and auto saloon No. 230 at Tavistock, before alighting at Marsh Mills Station and thinking how sad it was that we would never again travel over the entire branch as it had been on that day.

One further, shorter trip is worth recording as my last journey of any length on the line, although it was not intended as such. On 8th December the family travelled from Marsh Mills to Tavistock on the 3.12 p.m. train, which was made up of 2–6–2T No. 5568 and two corridor coaches. Before we left, two lighted hurricane lamps were loaded onto the train and, in true branch line fashion, these were hung out at Plym Bridge Platform. Four more were collected at Bickleigh, of which two were hung out at Shaugh Bridge Platform and two at Clearbrook Halt.

After a look around Tavistock, we boarded the 6.40 p.m. train (which was our outward one, returning from Launceston); it was now dark, with the moon appearing every so often through gaps in the clouds. One abiding memory is of crossing Grenofen viaduct and seeing the River Walkham far below, gleaming in the moonlight.

At Horrabridge we crossed 2–6–2T No. 4591 on a two-coach train and later alighted at Marsh Mills, which, as events transpired, would be for the last time on the 'up' platform.

Christmas 1962 was spent with my parents at Torquay, and we were still there on the closing day of the Launceston branch; this was Saturday, 29th December, as no trains were timetabled on Sundays. However, as I was anxious to witness the 'last rites' on the line, I left the family in Torquay and caught a train (a three-car diesel multiple unit set) that took me through to Plymouth (North Road) Station by 11.45 a.m., with no change at Newton Abbot, which was a good start to the day. I then waited around and presently saw the 10.15 a.m. train from Launceston arrive at 12.08 p.m., some seventeen minutes late and consisting of 2–6–2T No. 5569 and four corridor coaches. The locomotive carried a wreath of flowers, donated by the Plymouth Railway Circle, on its offside lamp bracket, but this was then removed by the fireman and passed to a member of the Circle for use on other branch trains during the day.

I now intended to move on to Marsh Mills Station in order to watch the afternoon train movements and so, with this in mind and in preparation for my final journey along the branch later in the day, I purchased two return tickets. The first was to Marsh Mills and the second was to Launceston, the fares being 1/4d. (7p) and 7/3d. (36p) respectively. Having done that, I then joined the 12.45 p.m. branch service to Tavistock, which was being worked by 0–6–0PT No. 6400 (now carrying the P.R.C. wreath) and three coaches, and travelled, as planned, to Marsh Mills, where I alighted and waited to see the 1.15 p.m. train to Plymouth. The weather, meanwhile, was far from good, and by this time there

Two scenes at Marsh Mills Station on the last day of the branch passenger service, 29th December 1962:–
Top: The 2.17 p.m. train to Tavistock, in the charge of 0–6–0PT No. 6430.

Lower: The 2.6 p.m. train from Launceston, behind 2–6–2T No. 5564 (with the Plymouth Railway Circle's headboard on its bunker).

was a covering of snow everywhere. However, the 'up' train, composed of 0–6–0PT No. 6430, three auto saloons (Nos. 234 – 228 – 230) and converted passenger brake van No. 255, presently arrived and then, shortly afterwards, departed for Plymouth nine minutes behind schedule, at 1.24 p.m.

My next move was a quick visit home to Woodford in order to prepare lunch. I then returned to the station in time to see the 2.17 p.m. train to Tavistock, which was in the charge of 0–6–0PT No. 6430 and made up of the same four vehicles as before. Next was the train from Launceston, due at 2.06 p.m., but which arrived late behind 2–6–2T No. 5564 (now carrying the wreath and also a 'Farewell' board). This train, consisting of four corridor coaches, was well patronised and departed for Plymouth at 2.30 p.m., which, in turn, allowed the 2.17 p.m. 'down' train to leave at 2.31 p.m., albeit with only a small number of passengers on board.

Meanwhile, the snow continued to fall, and the worsening conditions were accentuated by high winds.

Another quick visit home enabled me to have a somewhat late lunch before returning to the station once again so as to see the 3.12 p.m. train to Launceston, which arrived late in thickly falling snow; it was headed by 2–6–2T No. 4591 (with the 'Farewell' board) and there were four carriages, each holding a large number of railway enthusiasts. After that, one last brief interval at home gave me time for a warming meal, and then it was back to Marsh Mills in order to catch the 5.7 p.m. train into Plymouth. By now it was dark, but the station lights were presently switched on and I waited in the doorway of the small waiting shelter on the 'up' platform. In the meantime, the weather had deteriorated still further, and, apart from one lady waiting for the 5.32 p.m. train on the 'down' platform, there were no other passengers about.

My train eventually drew into the platform at 5.32 p.m. and was the same one – 0–6–0PT No. 6430 and its four coaches – that I had already seen on two previous occasions during the course of the afternoon. I then climbed aboard, noticing that members of the Plymouth Railway Circle were included amongst the passengers, and we pulled out at 5.41 p.m. after a brief delay caused by frozen points.

Out on the main line we passed the 'down' train (0–6–0PT No. 6400 and three corridor coaches) that had been due at Marsh Mills at 5.32 p.m., and went on to reach North Road Station at 5.49 p.m. After alighting, I then crossed over to platforms 7 and 8 in order to await the 6.20 p.m. train to Launceston. However, it soon became apparent that a really bitter wind was blowing along the platforms and so, with no sign of the train appearing, I sought some shelter behind the bookstall for a while.

When the train did at long last draw in, at platform 6, it was a welcome relief to climb into the relative warmth of one of its four coaches, which were being hauled by 2–6–2T No. 5568. After that, we finally departed at 7.32 p.m. (well over an hour late!), with no whistles or detonators or even spectators to wave us off, and got as far as Laira, where we were held up by signals; we then briefly restarted, only to be held again somewhere near Crabtree.

After a while, with the snow now being driven horizontally past the train and the water in the Laira estuary having become very rough, the guard came along the train saying that we would try to reach Marsh Mills but doubted if we would get any further as points were frozen. On hearing this, and taking into account the fact that it was already around 8.30 p.m., I decided to abandon my journey and make for home, so I informed the guard, who warned me that it was at my own risk. He then asked for my ticket and appeared to agree with me that it was a good idea.

Moments later I got down onto the lineside, climbed through the fence and started to walk along the route of the Lee Moor Tramway, leaving the train standing there with the front of the locomotive, complete with its wreath, becoming white with the driving snow. The walk through the blizzard was not easy, but I eventually reached Marsh Mills Station, where I saw a four-coach train standing alongside the 'up' platform. Then, when I went up to them, the locomotive crew told me they were on the 5.40 p.m. service from Launceston and had managed to get this far with great difficulty due to frozen points and snowdrifts partly blocking the line in places. The engine was the 'old faithful' 2–6–2T No. 4591: the 'Farewell' board was in place on the bunker (she had been travelling in reverse) and the rear bogie was caked with snow from where she had forced her way through the drifts.

Apart from the passenger train, I also saw an 'up' freight train in a siding, in the charge of 2–6–2T No. 4574. However, I now left both trains standing there in driving wind and snow, lit by the orange vapour lamps from the road and the station lights, and walked home, feeling sorry that my journey had had to be abandoned, but that the right decision had been made. As things transpired, I realised that it certainly had!

101

My train had eventually managed to reach Tavistock after midnight, whilst No. 4591 had brought her coaches into North Road Station at about 10.30 p.m. In addition, the 7.10 p.m. train from Tavistock had been held at Bickleigh, and remained there, completely frozen up.

The rest of the story of that epic night has been told elsewhere, but for those who witnessed the events it will remain an unforgettable memory.

The next morning I walked past Marsh Mills Station, where No. 4574 was still in the siding with her train, the locomotive 'dead', and on through the snow-covered streets to North Road Station. Here I boarded a waiting train at 9.30 a.m., which I hoped would take me to Newton Abbot.

It eventually pulled out at 12.30 p.m. and, after being delayed by a snowdrift near Ivybridge, reached Newton Abbot at 2.30 p.m. No trains appeared to be running on the Kingswear branch, but a Devon General bus took me to Torquay and I finally reached my parents' house at 5.10 p.m. at the end of a somewhat unusual journey!

As for the Launceston branch in the days that followed, part of the northern section of the line remained open for milk and other freight traffic for a few more years, but this ceased in 1966, and the whole of the route was dismantled.

The portion from Plym Bridge to beyond Shaugh tunnel (with a break at Bickleigh) is now a 'Sustrans' foot and cycle path, whilst the Plym Valley Railway Company is endeavouring to reopen the section from near Marsh Mills Station to Plym Bridge as a tourist line. In addition, at the time of writing, china clay is still being taken from the works near Marsh Mills to the main line. However, the china clay company has recently announced that the works at Lee Moor are scheduled for possible closure, which would mean the cessation of this traffic.

It appears, therefore, that apart from the section being restored by the Plym Valley Railway Company, the line to Tavistock and Launceston will soon be only a memory, although the magnificent viaducts at Riverford and Bickleigh, in particular, will remain as fitting memorials.

✳✳✳✳✳

6. THE TEIGN VALLEY BRANCH

The Teign Valley branch, like the Brixham and Moretonhampstead branches, was one of the local railways which I first explored with a school friend on Saturday mornings in the latter half of the 1930s.

It had been opened in two stages, the first in 1882 from Heathfield Station on the Moretonhampstead branch to a station at Ashton, with a freight-only line continuing to Teign House, and the second in 1903 from Teign House (renamed 'Christow') to the main GWR line just south of Exeter St Thomas Station at City Basin Junction.

A journey along the branch in the 'down' direction commenced from one of the platforms at Exeter St David's Station, from where the main line was followed to Exeter St Thomas Station (74 chains) and on to City Basin Junction (1 mile 19 chains). Here the branch train crossed the 'up' main line to reach Teign Valley line metals and, after passing a trailing connection to Alphington Road Goods Yard, soon reached Alphington Halt (2 miles 1 chain). This timber-built platform with a waiting shelter was sited on the left-hand

Alphington Halt, 22nd June 1950.

103

side of the line, and from here the locomotive faced a winding climb of almost 4 miles to reach the line's summit.

In just over a mile from Alphington Halt the train arrived at Ide Halt (3 miles 19 chains), a curving platform on the right-hand side of the line with a brick building which denoted its former status as a station. Beyond the halt, with the gradient rising at 1 in 58, the

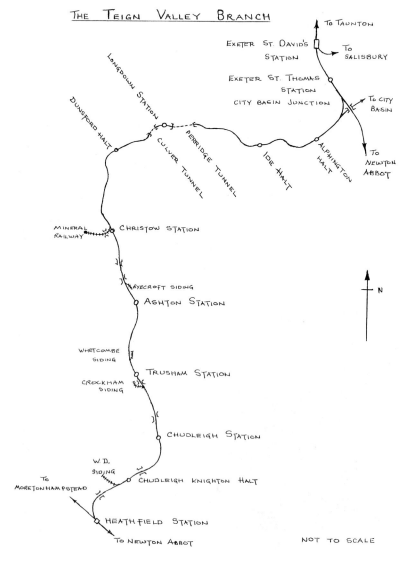

train passed through a wooded valley and, after threading Perridge tunnel (836 yards), emerged at the head of another valley as it arrived at Longdown Station (5 miles 77 chains). Situated some 400 feet above sea level in a remote setting away from roads, this also had a curving platform on the right-hand side of the line with a brick station building, but, in addition, had a signal box

Ide Halt, 10th June 1957.

Longdown Station, 21st July 1950.

which stood immediately beyond the far (western) end of the platform.

Having climbed to the summit of the branch, the train now started to descend on a gradient of 1 in 64 and entered a tunnel as it approached Cotley Wood. This was Culver tunnel (248 yards), from where the train soon emerged to run along the shoulder of a hill towards Dunsford Halt (7 miles 20 chains), a little-used stopping place on the left-hand side of the line with a short platform and corrugated iron shelter.

Dunsford Halt, 21st July 1950.

Just beyond the halt, the line curved quite sharply around to the south, but continued to run along the shoulder of the hill for about another mile until entering the valley of the River Teign near Bridfordmills. After that, the train soon reached Christow Station (9 miles 22 chains), which was the largest and most important intermediate stopping point along the branch, incorporating both 'up' and 'down' platforms, a passing loop, quite a sizeable signal box and watering facilities. The main station building, constructed of red brick under a hipped roof, was situated on the 'up' platform, immediately adjacent to a goods shed, and there was a small waiting shelter of matching red brick directly opposite, on the 'down' platform, next to a water crane. A goods yard, where the facilities included a cattle dock, was sited on the Exeter side of the 'up' platform, and for some years there was a connection off one of

Christow Station, 23rd June 1950.

A somewhat busier scene at Christow Station, on 26th May 1958, as 2–6–2T No. 5558 and 0–6–0PT No. 3606 wait for the 'off' with the 1.16 p.m. train to Exeter and the 1.17 p.m. train to Heathfield respectively.

the sidings here to a short private mineral railway which served the quarries of the Devon Basalt and Granite Company. In addition, an aerial ropeway carrying skip-type buckets brought stone down from Scatter Rock Quarry to be loaded into railway wagons from hoppers on the 'down' side of the line.

Southwards of Christow the gradients eased considerably and the train followed a much less winding course, initially keeping to the east of the river until presently crossing it, only to then recross it almost at once. Here, on the left-hand side of the line, was a siding serving Ryecroft Quarry (10 miles 29 chains), after which it was only a short distance to a gated level crossing which carried the line over the road leading to Lower and Higher Ashton immediately before the train entered the confines of Ashton Station (10 miles 68 chains); this consisted of a single, curving platform on the right-hand side of the line with a yellow brick station building and a brick-built ground frame on the opposite side, just inside the level-crossing gates. It also had a small goods yard that extended southwards from behind the platform, and opposite this stood the long-disused locomotive shed of the original line.

The train now remained on the eastern side of the river for almost 2 miles, passing a further siding at Whetcombe Quarry (12 miles 33 chains) on the left before reaching Trusham Station

Ashton Station, 23rd June 1950.

Trusham Station, 23rd June 1950.

(12 miles 63 chains). Here, the main station building was virtually identical to that at Ashton and, once again, was sited on the right-hand side of the line. There was also a small goods yard that, similarly, extended southwards from behind the platform but, unlike Ashton, Trusham boasted a signal box (situated just beyond the southern end of the platform), a passing loop and, from 1943 onwards, a second ('down') platform.

Shortly after leaving Trusham the train crossed to the western side of the river and passed a siding on the right-hand side of the line at 13 miles 8 chains, which led back to a level crossing over the main Teign Valley road (the B3193) and continued to the crushers of the nearby Crockham Quarry.

Further down the valley, the river was crossed for the fourth time before the train approached the next station at Chudleigh (14 miles 51 chains). However, just before it entered the station, and on slightly higher ground, the train passed an unusual feature on the left-hand side of the line, which took the form of a raised wooden gangway with white-painted railings. Connected to a nearby lane, this was an alternative means of joining or leaving a train if the station was flooded by the river, which did occur on rare occasions.

The station itself was situated immediately on the far side of a

109

bridge under the main Exeter to Plymouth road and consisted of a platform on the left-hand side of the line with station buildings of wooden construction, plus a small goods yard which, like those at Ashton and Trusham, extended southwards from behind the platform.

Chudleigh Station, 15th June 1950.

Chudleigh Knighton Halt, 10th June 1957.

In another mile the river was crossed for the fifth and final time before the train reached a level crossing over a lane and arrived at Chudleigh Knighton Halt (15 miles 74 chains), a single platform with a pagoda shelter on the right-hand side of the line. In contrast to the majority of stopping places on the branch, and with the exception of Ide, this one was quite close to the village after which it was named.

Now on the last part of its journey, the train again passed under the A38 main road before crossing, in quick succession, a corner of Chudleigh Knighton Heath, the River Bovey and a level crossing over a minor road. The final few yards were on a sharp left-hand curve with a rising gradient, bringing the train to rest alongside the north-eastern face of the 'up' platform at Heathfield Station (17 miles 3 chains).

The Teign Valley bay platform at Heathfield Station, showing 0–4–2T No. 1469 and auto saloons Nos. 96 and 93 about to depart on the 1.20 p.m. service to Exeter, 1st April 1950.

My own acquaintance with the branch, as previously stated, began in the latter part of the 1930s, but I regret that the only recorded detail of those days is of seeing two trains on 27th February 1939, each consisting of a single auto saloon and being headed by 2–4–0T No. 3587 and 0–4–2T No. 4851 respectively.

Journeys on the line in those days always started from my 'home' station of Torre, and after changing trains at Heathfield we would alight either at Chudleigh, Trusham, Ashton or Christow. Anywhere further was out of our reach on a Saturday morning trip, and would, in any event, have exceeded our weekly pocket money!

As on other lines, the fares in those days now seem unbelievable, ranging from 1/10d. (9p) day return to Chudleigh to 2/4d. (12p) to Christow. These were full adult fares – up to the age of 14 (or was it 16?) we travelled at half that amount.

111

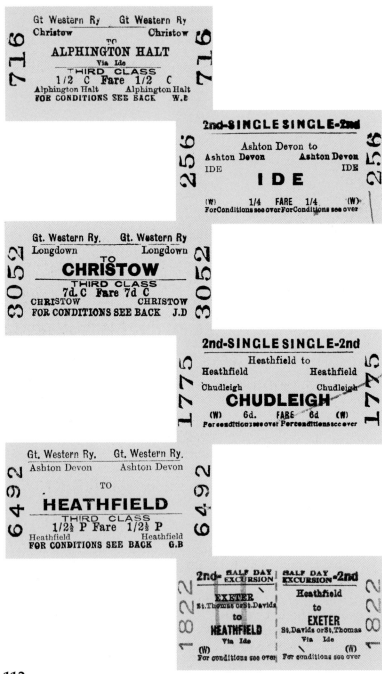

I do not recollect ever alighting at Chudleigh Knighton Halt, but at Chudleigh we would walk up to the town, looking out along the way for Chudleigh Rocks and Caves, which we never did discover. Trusham was more interesting, with the siding to Crockham Quarry crossing the main Teign Valley road, and sometimes there would be wagons being shunted from the crushers by travelling steam cranes.

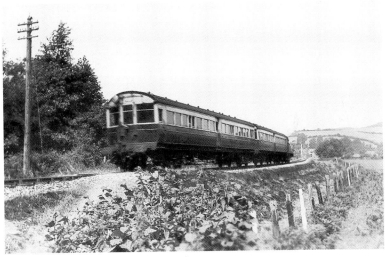

A train bound for Heathfield soon after leaving Ashton Station on 28th June 1952, with 0–4–2T No. 1451 propelling auto saloons Nos. 155 and 215.

Ashton was a pleasant spot, with the road up to Higher Ashton and also the ancient Spara Bridge over the river. However, the favourite destination was Christow, for here we could watch the buckets moving along the aerial ropeway, bringing stone from Scatter Rock Quarry to railway wagons waiting in the sidings. There was also the route of the former private tramway to the quarries of the Devon Basalt and Granite Company to look at. (This had been closed and the track lifted some years before our visits, and on the first search for its course we wandered up a private lane, to be met by a gentleman who enquired where we were going. When we explained, he said "you mean the old mineral line" and pointed us in the right direction. However, there was very little to be seen, as the route had been converted to a road, but I do remember seeing the ends of rails in the edge of the tarmac at the side of the main road. There was also a low

113

embankment leading to what had been a bridge used to carry the line over the river on a curve just before reaching the goods yard of Christow Station. The bridge, though, was now no more than a few rotting timbers linking seven piers sunk into the bed of the river.)

In those years before, during and after the Second World War most of the branch passenger trains were hauled by the '48xx' (later '14xx') class 0–4–2T locomotives, including Nos. 4805 – 4829 – 4835 – 4839 – 4840 – 4849 – 4851 – 4868 and 4869. There were exceptions, such as on 29th September 1941, when 2–4–0T No. 3581 was noted with auto saloon No. 155, and again on 5th February 1944, when 2–6–2T No. 5502 was recorded with auto saloon No. 157.

My most unusual sighting occurred on 24th February 1945 whilst waiting for a 'down' train at Ashton Station, as when the 6.24 p.m. 'up' train from Heathfield drew into the platform it was headed by 4–4–0 No. 3451 *Pelican* (with auto saloon No. 146) – there must have been some unforeseen happenings in the motive power department on that day! Incidentally my train, which would have crossed the other one at Christow, arrived at 6.58 p.m. to take me to Heathfield and was made up of 2–6–2T No. 5543 coupled to two auto saloons, Nos. 156 and 139.

There were a number of other auto saloons used on the Teign Valley trains during this period, including Nos. 22 – 132 – 138 – 147 – 149 –193 – 215 – 222 – 224 and 240, and occasionally Nos. 96 and 93, which I suspect may have been on a through working from the Exe Valley line.

Sometime in 1943 I noted that a fan of three sidings with a trailing connection to 'up' trains had been installed on Chudleigh Knighton Heath to serve a nearby American military storage depôt. Soon after D–Day, however, the sidings fell into disuse and were taken out again some years before the line's closure.

One of the popular destinations for our Church's Youth Guild rambles was Steps Bridge, higher up the Teign Valley, and on 10th April 1944 we started by boarding the 10.15 a.m. train from Torre Station. This consisted of a specially strengthened Bank Holiday formation with auto saloon No. 158 ahead of 0–4–2T No. 1427 and auto coaches Nos. 3275 and 3331 at the rear. We rode on it as far as Heathfield, where we changed to the Teign Valley train, with 0–4–2T No. 4849 hauling auto saloons Nos. 147 and 215, and this took us on to Christow Station. We were then faced with a walk of some 3 miles, all along roads, to reach Steps Bridge – it seems a long way now, but we didn't seem to notice in those days!

Trains crossing at Christow Station. In this photograph, taken on 12th April 1952, the train on the left is the 1.30 p.m. (Saturdays only) to Exeter – made up of auto saloons Nos. 96 and 93 and 0–4–2T No. 1468 – while the other is the 1.28 p.m. to Heathfield, with 0–4–2T No. 1449 propelling auto saloon No. 149.

After a day by the river, and admiring the wild daffodils which grew on its banks, we returned to Christow Station to catch the 6.52 p.m. train back to Heathfield, riding in single auto saloon No. 156 propelled by 0–4–2T No. 4869. (I think it was on this trip that I noticed for the first time that a new concrete platform with a waiting shelter had been installed beside the 'down' loop line at Trusham Station.)

The excursion was repeated some years later, and those Bank Holiday trips are among my happiest memories of the line.

I did eventually travel the whole of the line, one occasion being on 21st April 1945 when returning home for weekend leave whilst serving in the Army at Portland. On reaching Exeter St David's Station (after coming down the Southern Railway line from Yeovil Junction), I discovered that the next train to Newton Abbot was via the Teign Valley line, so decided to travel that way. The train that evening was composed of 2–6–2T No. 5543 hauling auto saloon No. 147 and non-corridor clerestory coach No. 7135.

After returning to civilian life in 1948, I resumed my visits to the branch and found that the stone traffic from the Whetcombe and

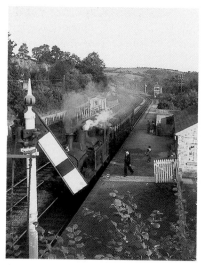

A view of Trusham Station on 28th August 1954 as 0–4–2T No. 1468 and auto saloon No. 138 depart with the 6.33 p.m. service to Exeter.

Ryecroft quarries must have ceased some time previously as both sidings were noted as 'disused and overgrown' in March of that year.

Most of the trains still consisted of 0–4–2T locomotives (now renumbered in the '14xx' series) with auto saloons, an exception being an evening train from Exeter on 18th April 1949, which I joined at Christow, as this was being hauled by 0–6–0PT No. 7716.

Up until 21st July 1950 I had never alighted at, or caught a train from, either Dunsford Halt or Longdown Station, but on that day I set out with a friend to remedy this omission.

We began by catching the 3.5 p.m. train from platform 9 at Newton Abbot, which was a through service via the Teign Valley line to Exeter being worked by 0–4–2T No. 1405 and auto saloon No. 157.

After alighting at Longdown, we surrendered the 'outward' portion of our tickets and ascended the footpath behind the station building to reach an unmade farm lane which, in turn, took us out onto the main Exeter to Moretonhampstead road. There was no footpath here, but we walked on towards Longdown village until presently turning into a lane which eventually led us us (in a circular route) to Dunsford

The approach to Perridge tunnel, viewed from the platform of Longdown Station on 1st February 1958.

Halt. (If we had been residents of Longdown village, we would still have had some distance to walk from the point where we left the main road to reach our home, so it was not surprising that the station saw very few passengers.)

Our return train from the halt arrived at 6.49 p.m., with 0–4–2T No. 1449 hauling auto saloons Nos. 132 and 22 – it was quite a relief to relax on the cushions as we travelled back down the valley, and, needless to say, we had been the only passengers at both Longdown Station and Dunsford Halt!

Over the next few years I continued to visit the line at intervals and noted that after 1957 the auto saloons no longer appeared on the trains, my last sighting being of No. 215 (with 0–4–2T No. 1405) at Chudleigh Knighton Halt on 10th June 1957.

Auto saloon No. 215 and 0–4–2T No. 1405 leaving Chudleigh Knighton Halt with the 10.50 a.m. service to Exeter on 10th June 1957.

117

One of the 0–6–0PT locomotives, No. 3606, seen with two corridor coaches soon after leaving Heathfield Station with the 4.44 p.m. service to Exeter on 31st May 1958.

From then onwards the trains I saw were composed of two coaches, usually corridor vehicles, attached to a '45xx' class 2–6–2T or an 0–6–0PT; occasionally, I also saw one of the familiar '14xx' class 0–4–2T locomotives providing the motive power, but again with two coaches.

Notices proposing closure of the branch appeared around June 1957 and this prompted me to visit some of the stations in order to purchase tickets as souvenirs: at Longdown I was not greatly surprised when the gentleman in charge there told me that mine was the first ticket he had sold for a week!

At the beginning of 1958 it was announced that the passenger service would cease as from Monday, 3rd March, but due to local objections the date was postponed to Monday, 9th June, which meant that the final trains would run on the preceding Saturday, the 7th. It was also announced that on this date the section from Christow (exclusive) to City Basin Junction would be closed to all traffic except for a short length of track at the Exeter end leading to the Marsh Barton Trading Estate near Alphington.

In order to see as much as possible of the events on that rather sad day my family and I travelled by car up the valley, as far as Christow, watching the trains at various locations and taking photographs.

Facing page: The last day of passenger services, showing 2–6–2T No. 5536 leaving Heathfield Station with the 10.43 a.m. train to Exeter (top), 0–4–2T No. 1451 with the 12.49 p.m. train from Heathfield at Christow Station (centre) and 2–6–2T No. 5530 with the 4.44 p.m. from Heathfield at Trusham Station (lower).

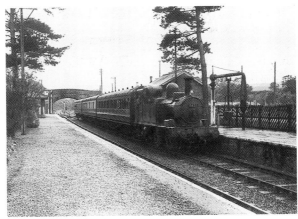

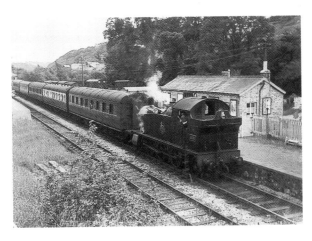

Most of the trains carried a good complement of passengers, and included 2–6–2T No. 5536 with three coaches, 0–4–2T No. 1451 with three coaches, and also 2–6–2T No. 5530 with five coaches. One unexpected sighting was a camping coach, which appeared to be occupied, in the siding at Chudleigh Station.

In the early evening we left the car at Newton Abbot and joined a crowd of people on platform 9 in order to travel on the final 'up' train through the valley, which was due to leave at 8.0 p.m.

At 7.25 p.m. the 'down' working drew in, with a rather grubby 2–6–2T, No. 5533, hauling two coaches packed with passengers. After they had alighted, the locomotive reversed the train out of the platform, ran around her coaches and waited whilst four more coaches were shunted into the platform. The other two coaches were then brought back and coupled up, making a six-coach train (Nos. 5231 – 5077 – 2196 – 6214 – 5713 – 2159) headed by 2–6–2T No. 5533 (bunker first).

Passengers boarded the train, which was soon quite well filled, but not crowded, and we pulled out four minutes late at 8.4 p.m. No stop was made at Teigngrace, and at Heathfield the train used the 'down' platform, where a small crowd was waiting. Several boarded the train, and we left at 8.13 p.m., rounding the curve onto the Teign Valley line and soon reaching Chudleigh Knighton Halt, where a handful of people were waiting. Several passengers alighted here, and this meant that the train had to stop twice to allow them to reach the short platform, losing a little more time. Chudleigh Station was quite crowded, but there were not many at Trusham; however, the platform at Ashton was well filled and a number entrained, including a gentleman with a bugle. We had to stop twice here, and eventually departed, now twelve minutes late, to a bugle fanfare, which was repeated at all subsequent stations and 'en route' as well!

The residents of the Christow area were on the platform in large numbers, and we left with a full train at 8.48 p.m., having lost a further four minutes due to the extended stop.

The locomotive climbed steadily up to Dunsford Halt, where four people joined the train and two alighted, but the gradient and the heavy train caused some slipping as we restarted; however, the second attempt was successful and the ascent continued up to and through Culver tunnel to the remote Longdown Station, where, surprisingly, four people were waiting. After leaving again at 9.4 p.m. (now nineteen minutes late), we passed through Perridge tunnel and made a restrained descent to Ide Halt, where a small group greeted the train. At the final branch platform, Alphington Halt, quite a number alighted, and we pulled out at 9.18 p.m., now twenty-two minutes late. Further time was lost as we were held up twice at City Basin Junction, and then at Exeter St Thomas (where no-one was waiting) we made our last call before drawing into the former Southern Railway 'down' platform at Exeter St David's at 9.33 p.m., just twenty-eight minutes late.

A crowd was waiting to greet the train here, and whilst some were singing 'Auld Lang Syne' flowers were laid on the running plate of the locomotive. She presently ran around her train, the passengers rejoined the coaches, and the final journey began, with a small crowd to bid us farewell, at 9.54 p.m., just twenty-four minutes after the booked time of 9.30 p.m.

At Exeter St Thomas we collected a few more passengers before joining the branch at City Basin Junction, whilst several more boarded at Alphington Halt. People were waving to the train from their gardens by the line as the daylight began to fade, and No. 5533 faced the long climb ahead. At Ide Halt quite a crowd was there to greet us and then, as darkness fell, we forged slowly but steadily upwards, with someone waving a torch from a nearby farm. After running through the tunnel, and having quite a long stop at Longdown Station, which was out of sight from our coach, we restarted with a two-tone whistle from No. 5533, and a bugle fanfare, at 10.29 p.m. By now we were thirty-seven minutes late!

The descent to Dunsford Halt was taken cautiously and then we stopped at the empty platform; no-one alighted, but three people leaning on a nearby farm gate saw our train pass for the last time.

Down at Christow, lit by oil lamps, many had gathered on the platform and now watched whilst our locomotive took a well-earned drink. The journey continued with several detonators exploding as we left at 10.50 p.m. – instead of at 10.1 p.m.!

At Ashton another crowd had turned out to see the train, and cars were stopped on each side of the level crossing. Our bugler departed here with a final burst of melody, and we ran on down the valley to Trusham, where, as on the outward trip, not many people had appeared to greet us.

Two stops were necessary at Chudleigh to allow passengers to detrain, and then, after pausing at Chudleigh Knighton Halt at 11.18 p.m., we reached Heathfield to again find people waiting to see us pass.

After leaving at 11.25 p.m., we ran non-stop to Newton Abbot, arriving at the main 'down' platform at 11.35 p.m., exactly one hour late after a memorable journey. The train was still quite full here and, after everyone had alighted, we climbed the station stairs feeling that we had said farewell to a railway which had given us much pleasure over the years, and which would be greatly missed.

As we left the station, No. 5533 slowly backed her train out of the station into the darkness and into history.

In the months that followed, the line retained a freight service from Heathfield as far as Christow, with the remainder of the route being dismantled; however, in early 1961 severe flooding breached the track between Ashton and Trusham, meaning that trains were then terminated at Trusham.

At the same time the South Devon Railway Society, an organisation which had hoped to take over the Moretonhampstead branch, had chartered a special excursion along the Teign Valley on 4th March, commencing from Newton Abbot and running to Christow. Consequently, although the train still ran, it could travel no further that Trusham.

Having persuaded my father to accompany me, we joined about fifty other persons on platform 9 at Newton Abbot at around 1.45 p.m. on the day, and found 2–6–2T No. 4174 standing there with her train of eight brake vans.

Departure was at 2.0 p.m., and we proceeded at a gentle pace to Teigngrace Halt, where the Society Chairman, Canon O. Jones, and his wife joined us. The train then continued to Heathfield, where we were allowed a ten-minute 'photo stop'.

After moving off again, we rounded the curve from the station, soon halting to allow the fireman to open, and the guard to close, the level-crossing gates at Bovey Lane. This exercise was then repeated at Chudleigh Knighton Halt, where only the platform remained, prior to us reaching Chudleigh Station, where it was obvious that the flood waters had eroded part of the platform surface.

We reached Trusham Station at 2.59 p.m., to find all the signals dismantled and the waiting shelter on the 'down' platform removed; the only sign of activity was a large number of wagons, including cement wagons, in the Crockham Quarry siding.

The locomotive then ran around her train, the passengers climbed aboard and we commenced the return journey at 3.42 p.m., stopping briefly at all stations and reaching Newton Abbot,

The South Devon Railway Society's brake van special approaching Chudleigh Knighton Halt on the return journey, 4th March 1961.

again at platform 9, at 4.35 p.m. It had been a very pleasant, unhurried ride in sunny weather, and my father was gracious enough to say that he had enjoyed the experience!

So ended my journeys by train along the Teign Valley, and subsequent visits to the area were made in the family car. I noted 0–6–0PT No. 3796 shunting wagons in the Crockham Quarry sidings on 6th May 1961 and a 'Large Prairie' 2–6–2T engaged in similar duties on 10th February 1964, this being my final sighting

123

of steam on the line. A month later, on 26th March, diesel locomotive D6331 was shunting tankers at Chudleigh Station, and that was to be my last-ever view of activity on the branch. The washed-out track was never reinstated and final closure of the remaining portion came at the end of 1967, completing the story of a line which had been constructed in two sections with a gap of twenty-one years in between. It had served as a vital relief route when rough seas closed the main line at Dawlish, and if still with us today could relieve at least some of the delays due to modern diesel-electric trains having a strong dislike of sea water!

In the intervening years since the closure many changes have occurred along the line's route, which has been severed in several places.

At Heathfield Station the two platforms remain in a derelict condition, with the rails of the Moretonhampstead line still in occasional use.

Chudleigh Knighton Halt and Chudleigh Station have both been swept away by the re-routed A38 main road, which has been constructed along the former track bed on that section of the line.

Further up the valley, the main station building at Trusham has been adapted as a holiday home, whilst those at Ashton and Christow stations have been converted to attractive, modern dwellings.

On the upper part of the line, the site of Dunsford Halt has become an overgrown corner of a field, whilst the station building at Longdown has been used as a store.

Approaching Exeter, Ide Halt has been demolished to make way for a modern housing development, and the location of Alphington Halt has become obscured by trees and undergrowth.

Elsewhere, it is still possible to see a length of the track bed here and there, and also the odd bridge or two over or under the route, but otherwise the Teign Valley line has become just another fond memory for those of us who enjoyed riding on its trains over forty years ago.

*****

BIBLIOGRAPHY

The Ashburton Branch

KAY, Peter, *The Ashburton Branch – A New History.* Published privately 2000
KINGDOM, Anthony R., *The Ashburton Branch (and The Totnes Quay Line).* Oxford Publishing Company 1977
KINGDOM, Anthony R., *The Totnes to Ashburton Railway (and The Totnes Quay Line).* ARK Publications (Railways) 1995

The Bodmin and Wadebridge Railway

FAIRCLOUGH, Tony & WILLS, Alan, *Bodmin and Wadebridge 1834 – 1978.* D. Bradford Barton 1979
WHETMATH, C. F. D., *The Bodmin & Wadebridge Railway.* Branch Line Handbooks/Westcountry Handbooks 1967

The Brixham Branch

DILLEY, John, *Mr Wolston's Little Line.* John Dilley Publishing 1990
POTTS, C. R., *The Brixham Branch.* The Oakwood Press 1986

The Kingsbridge Branch

WILLIAMS, Ken & REYNOLDS, Dermot, *The Kingsbridge Branch.* Oxford Publishing Co. 1977

The Launceston Branch

ANTHONY, G. H., *The Tavistock, Launceston & Princetown Railways.* The Oakwood Press 1971
KINGDOM, Anthony R., *The Plymouth Tavistock and Launceston Railway.* ARK Publications 1990
MILLS, Bernard, *The Branch: Plymouth – Tavistock South – Launceston.* Plym Valley Railway Company Ltd 1983

125

The Launceston Branch (continued)

ROCHE, T. W. E., *Plymouth and Launceston.* Branch-Line Handbooks 1965

The Teign Valley Branch

KAY, Peter, *The Teign Valley Line.* Wild Swan Publications Limited 1996
POMROY, L. W., *The Teign Valley Line.* Oxford Publishing Co. 1984
POMROY, Lawrence W., *The Heathfield to Exeter (Teign Valley) Railway.* ARK Publications (Railways) 1995

THE AUTHOR

Eric Shepherd was born in Torquay in 1924 and received his education at the local Boys' Grammar School.

His subsequent training as a Sanitary Inspector was interrupted by a period of three years' service with the Royal Engineers, two of which were spent in Egypt.

He completed his training after demobilisation and obtained a post with the Rochford Rural District Council in Essex, where he remained for four years.

After marrying and moving back to Devon, he continued his career in Local Government on the staff of the Plympton Rural District Council until retirement.

In recent years he has used his leisure time to research the history of some local railways.

He still lives near Plymouth and, apart from his lifelong interest in railways, enjoys exploring Dartmoor, bird watching and church organ music.

Eric R. Shepherd

Other Titles
available from
ARK Publications (Railways):–

Tavistock North & South
(Anthony R. Kingdom)

Brunel's Royal Albert Bridge
(Anthony R. Kingdom)

The Plymouth to Yealmpton Railway
(The South Hams Light Railway)
(Anthony R. Kingdom)

The Plymouth to Turnchapel Railway
(and The Cattewater Goods Line)
(Anthony R. Kingdom)

The Bombing of Newton Abbot Station
(Anthony R. Kingdom)

Growing Up on the Railway in the South West
(Grace Horseman)

The Heathfield to Exeter (Teign Valley) Railway
(Lawrence W. Pomroy)

The Plymouth Tavistock and Launceston Railway
(Anthony R. Kingdom)

The Newton Abbot to Moretonhampstead Railway
(Anthony R. Kingdom & Mike Lang)

The Railway Accident at Norton Fitzwarren, 1940
(Anthony R.Kingdom)

A Winter Remembered (Events recalling the winter of
1962/63 and its effect on the railways of Dartmoor)
(Robert E. Trevelyan)